Risk Reduction and Resilience

Plan to Ensure Long-term Business Survival and Success

The right of Jonathan Frost to be identified as the author of this work has been asserted in accordance with the copyright designs and patent Act 1988

drjonathanfrost.com

green-elephant.uk

ISBN: 9798336875478

Imprint: Independently published

All rights reserved. No part of this publication may be reproduced, stored in a retrieval system or transmitted in any form or by any means electronic, mechanical, photocopying, recording and/or otherwise without the prior written permission of the publishers. This book may not be lent, resold, hired out or otherwise disposed of by way of trading any form, binding or cover other than that in which it is published without the prior consent of the publishers.

Printed in UK by Amazon

Table of Contents

Preface 1

Chapter 1: Beyond Silos: Embracing the Complexity of Modern Risks 4

Chapter 2: The Proactive Imperative: Shifting the Paradigm in Risk Management 13

Chapter 3: Extreme Weather Events 24

Chapter 4: Social Instability 36

Chapter 5: Geoeconomic Confrontation 48

Chapter 6: Cybersecurity Threats 60

Chapter 7: Adverse Outcomes of Artificial Intelligence 73

Chapter 8: Cost-of-Living Crisis 84

Chapter 9: Infectious Disease Outbreaks 93

Chapter 10: Mis- and Disinformation 108

Chapter 11: Digital Inequality 121

Chapter 12: Human-Made Environmental Damage 133

Chapter 13: Natural Resource and Energy Crises 143

Chapter 14: Debt Crises, Demographics and Economic Shocks 153

Chapter 15: Risk Assessment Frameworks 166

Epilogue 176

References 179

Acknowledgements

I am happy and proud to acknowledge help and encouragement from Sean Vosler and the team at Movable Type

I would like to thank Martin Spence, Steve Shelley and Hans Christian Smith for many fruitful discussions.

Portrait photograph by Martyna Iwańska.

Dedication

*To My Growing Family - Lorraine, Peter, Ben,
Grace, Jodie, Jay, Emma, Ruben and Elora*

Preface

> *"In the midst of chaos, there is also opportunity."*
>
> *Sun Tzu*

The ancient wisdom of Sun Tzu reminds us that turbulence, while daunting, holds possibilities for those prepared to navigate through it. This book is crafted with the intent to arm you, the business leader, with the knowledge and tools necessary to transform global challenges into strategic opportunities.

At its core, this book provides a structured approach to mastering global risk management. It aims to equip senior executives, risk managers, and business leaders with the ability to identify, analyse, and mitigate the top global risks as outlined in the World Economic Forum's Global Risks Report 2024. The journey through these pages will take you from understanding broad risk concepts to applying specific strategies that fortify your organization against potential threats.

The impetus for writing this book stemmed from witnessing firsthand the struggles that leaders face in an ever-evolving risk landscape. Whether it was a conversation with a CEO who felt overwhelmed by the rapid technological changes impacting her company's operations, or a workshop with risk managers grappling with cybersecurity threats, these interactions highlighted a common theme: the need for a clear, actionable guide to navigating global risks.

Throughout my career, I've worn many hats—from teaching physics to inventing solutions for everyday problems. These experiences have not only broadened my perspective but have also ingrained in me a deep commitment to practical problem-solving. My role as an IT support provider further exposed me to the vulnerabilities businesses face from technological disruptions. This diversity of experience has shaped the pragmatic approach you'll find in this book.

I am indebted to numerous individuals who have enriched this project. Esteemed colleagues provided critical insights that have deepened the content's relevance and applicability. Friends and mentors offered encouragement and critique that were invaluable in refining my arguments.

As you turn these pages, remember that your time and attention are both precious. I appreciate your decision to engage with this work, and I trust it will prove beneficial as you steer your organization towards sustainability and success in a complex global environment.

This book is specifically designed for those at the helm of medium sized and large corporations, tasked with overseeing strategic foresight and corporate governance. It assumes a foundational understanding of business operations and strategic management. However, the concepts are presented in an accessible manner, ensuring clarity without sacrificing depth.

Thank you for choosing to explore these insights. I invite you now to delve deeper into each chapter, confident that the solutions you seek for tomorrow's challenges are within your grasp here today.

Chapter 1: Beyond Silos: Embracing the Complexity of Modern Risks

Learning Objective 1: Understand the limitations of managing risks in isolated categories.

Learning Objective 2: Explore the cascading effects of interconnected global risks on businesses.

Learning Objective 3: Identify strategies for creating a cohesive risk management approach that acknowledges interdependencies.

The late afternoon sun cast long shadows across the bustling streets of Singapore. Marcus stood by his office window, watching the city move in its perpetual rhythm. The recent geopolitical tensions in Eastern Europe had been a thorn in his side for weeks now, and he couldn't shake the feeling that more trouble was brewing just beyond the horizon.

He turned away from the window, his mind a whirlpool of thoughts. His company relied heavily on a supply chain that stretched from Asia to Europe and beyond. A disruption anywhere along this line could spell disaster. He thought back to last year when a sudden flood in Thailand had halted production for weeks. The financial hit

Risk Reduction and Resilience

had been significant, but it was the knock-on effects—the missed deadlines, the strained client relationships—that haunted him still.

The room smelled faintly of cedar from the polished wooden desk where he now sat, running his fingers over old reports and new projections. He recalled a conversation with Priya, his head of risk management, who had warned him about managing risks in silos. "It's like trying to stop a flood with sandbags," she had said. "You need to see how all these risks are interconnected."

Marcus sighed deeply and rubbed his temples. The interconnectedness of global risks wasn't just an abstract concept; it was a lived reality he grappled with every day. Environmental concerns weren't just about regulatory compliance—they impacted raw material costs and worker safety too. Technological advancements promised efficiency but also brought vulnerabilities that could be exploited by cyber threats.

His phone buzzed on the table, breaking his reverie. A message from Priya: "We need to discuss our new strategy—can't afford any weak links." Her words echoed in his mind as he thought about creating a more cohesive risk management approach—one that didn't just react to crises but anticipated them.

He stood up and paced around the room, feeling the cool breeze from the air conditioner against his skin. Outside, life went on as usual—people laughed at cafes, children played in parks—but Marcus knew that under this veneer of normalcy lay complexities that could unravel everything if not properly managed.

Could there ever be a truly sustainable business model that accounted for environmental consciousness, global supply chain resilience, workforce well-being, and post-growth principles? Or was this an unattainable ideal in an increasingly chaotic world?

Why Your Risk Management Needs a Rethink

In an era where global risks are intricately interwoven, traditional methods of managing risks in isolated silos fall short. The fragmented approach of categorizing risks into environmental, geopolitical, or technological domains no longer holds up against the complexities of today's world. **A disruption in one sector can swiftly trigger a domino effect**, leading to vulnerabilities in seemingly unrelated areas. This chapter sets the stage for understanding why an interconnected approach to risk management is not just beneficial but essential for businesses aiming to navigate tomorrow's turbulence.

The old model of compartmentalizing risks—treating environmental threats separately from geopolitical tensions or technological vulnerabilities—creates blind spots that can be perilous for modern enterprises. For instance, consider how geopolitical instability in a key region can disrupt supply chains globally, leading to economic fallout and even environmental degradation as companies scramble for alternative resources. **Managing these risks in silos ignores the cascading effects that a single disruption can have across multiple facets of a business.**

To create a cohesive risk management approach that acknowledges interdependencies, businesses must adopt new strategies. This involves not just identifying potential threats but also understanding how they interact with each other. **Developing cross-functional teams and fostering open communication channels** across departments can significantly improve an organization's ability to anticipate and mitigate complex risks.

Understanding the Limitations of Isolated Risk Management

The Interconnected Risk Landscape Model

This model serves as a strategic tool for mapping out the complex web of modern risks. It begins by identifying primary risk categories such as geopolitical, economic, environmental, technological, and societal factors.

Geopolitical Risks: These include issues like political instability or international conflicts which directly impact global trade policies and regulatory environments.

Risk Reduction and Resilience

Economic Risks: These encompass factors such as market fluctuations and financial crises which can destabilize economies globally.

Environmental Risks: These involve natural disasters and climate change impacts which not only cause immediate damage but also long-term disruptions to supply chains and living conditions.

Technological Risks: These include cyber threats and tech failures which pose growing challenges in our increasingly digital world.

Societal Risks: These refer to social unrest or demographic shifts which can alter consumer behaviour and influence global markets.

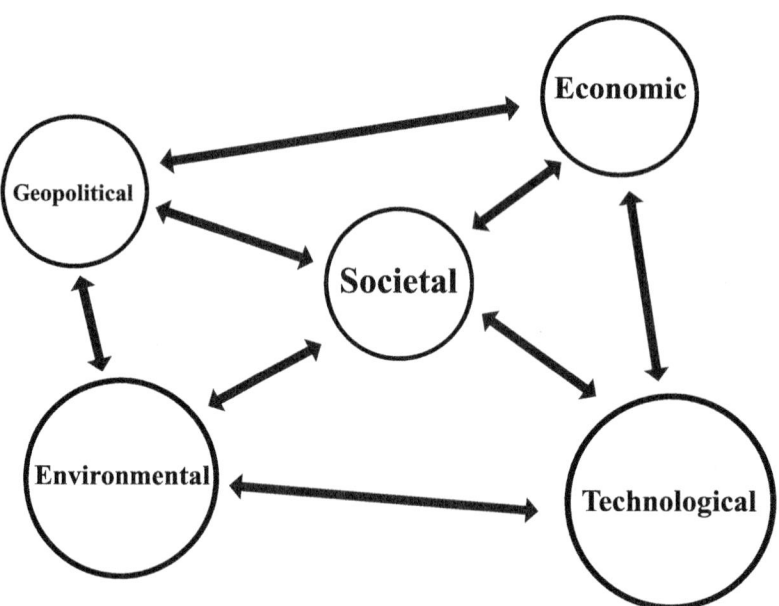

Each category is depicted as nodes within a network diagram in our model, with arrows indicating the potential ripple effects from one risk to another.

- A technological failure could lead to economic downturns due to halted production.
- Political unrest might exacerbate environmental issues if governance over natural resources becomes compromised.

Practical Implications

Employing this model allows businesses not just to react defensively but also proactively engage with potential threats before they manifest into crises. It encourages companies to:

- Conduct comprehensive risk assessments that account for cross-domain impacts.
- Develop integrated response strategies that address multiple outcomes simultaneously.
- Foster adaptability within organizational structures so they can pivot quickly in response to changing circumstances.

Ultimately, this model isn't just about avoiding threats—it's about enhancing strategic foresight and building enduring resilience within complex environments.

Risk Reduction and Resilience

By embracing an interconnected approach towards risk management that acknowledges every thread of the tapestry we call global business operations, companies not only protect themselves but also turn potential vulnerabilities into opportunities for growth and innovation.

Understanding the limitations of managing risks in isolated categories is the first step toward acknowledging the intricate web of interdependencies that define our modern world. Each risk, whether environmental, geopolitical, or technological, doesn't exist in a vacuum; it interacts with and influences other risks. As we've explored, these cascading effects can have profound impacts on businesses, underscoring the necessity of a holistic approach to risk management.

By embracing a cohesive strategy that recognizes these interconnections, businesses can better prepare for and mitigate the myriad challenges they face. This isn't just about survival; it's about thriving in an environment where change is constant and unpredictability is the norm. **A fragmented approach leaves organizations vulnerable**, while a comprehensive perspective equips them to navigate complexities with greater agility and resilience.

Incorporating strategies that account for interdependencies isn't merely an operational shift—it's a paradigm change. Businesses that succeed in this endeavour will not only protect their interests but also contribute to a more sustainable global ecosystem. This means being environmentally conscious, ensuring robust global supply chains, enhancing workforce quality of life, and adopting a post-growth mentality.

As we move forward in this book, you'll discover actionable insights and practical knowledge tailored to help you master global risk management. We'll delve into diverse perspectives and interdisciplinary approaches, ensuring you have a well-rounded understanding of how to build resilience in your organization. From real-life examples to innovative solutions, each chapter will equip you with tools to tackle tomorrow's turbulence confidently.

Are you ready to transform your approach to risk management? By embracing complexity and interconnectivity, you're setting the stage for long-term success and sustainability. Let's embark on this journey together—your future self will thank you.

Reflections

1. How does complexity impact our strategic objectives, and what steps are we taking to manage or leverage this complexity?

2. What are the primary drivers of complexity within our organization, and how do they influence our risk profile?

3. How do we ensure that our risk management framework is adaptable enough to respond to emerging complexities and risks?

4. What mechanisms do we have in place to assess the interdependencies of risks created by complexity, and how effective are they?

5. How do we balance the need for innovation with the potential risks introduced by increased complexity in our operations?

Chapter 2: The Proactive Imperative: Shifting the Paradigm in Risk Management

Learning Objective 1: Contrast reactive and proactive risk management methodologies.

Learning Objective 2: Examine the importance of incorporating forward-looking strategies into business planning.

Learning Objective 3: Develop skills for identifying and mitigating emerging threats proactively.

The sun had barely risen over the sleepy town of Fairview, casting a soft golden hue on the quiet streets. Jane walked briskly to the corner café, her mind racing ahead of her. The aroma of freshly brewed coffee mingled with the crisp morning air, offering a momentary distraction from her thoughts. She greeted the barista with a nod and ordered her usual—black coffee, no sugar. The warmth of the cup seeped through her fingers as she took a seat by the window.

Jane's company had been blindsided by a sudden supply chain disruption last month, and she couldn't shake off the lingering frustration. Her boss had called it an "unforeseeable event," but Jane knew better. They had relied too heavily on reactive risk management, always playing catch-up with problems instead of

Risk Reduction and Resilience

anticipating them. As she sipped her coffee, she thought back to that heated board meeting where she first suggested incorporating climate change projections into their business planning.

"Why should we worry about something that might happen decades from now?" one executive had scoffed.

Jane's fingers tightened around her cup as she recalled his dismissive tone. They didn't see what she saw—the slow but steady march of environmental changes that could cripple their operations if left unchecked. She believed in proactive risk management, identifying threats before they materialized and finding ways to mitigate them early on. But convincing others was another battle entirely.

Her phone buzzed on the table, pulling her out of her reverie. It was an email from Tom in logistics—a new report detailing potential emerging threats for their global supply chain over the next five years. Jane opened it eagerly, scanning through projections and data points that confirmed what she'd feared: rising sea levels threatening coastal suppliers, political instability in key regions, and shifting consumer demands toward more sustainable products.

She took another sip of coffee and let out a sigh. If only they had heeded her warnings earlier; they wouldn't be scrambling now to find alternative suppliers or reconfigure their distribution routes.

Risk Reduction and Resilience

A young couple entered the café, laughing softly as they shared an inside joke. Their carefree demeanour contrasted sharply with Jane's inner turmoil. She watched them for a moment before returning to Tom's email. They were looking for solutions now—better late than never—but how much smoother would things have been if they'd adopted forward-looking strategies from the start?

As Jane typed out a response to Tom, outlining potential action plans and pre-emptive measures they could take, she felt a glimmer of hope amidst her frustration. Maybe this time they'd listen; maybe this time they'd understand that proactive risk management wasn't just about avoiding crises but building resilience against future disruptions.

She hit send and leaned back in her chair, watching as sunlight filtered through the windowpane onto her table. Was it possible for one person's vision to shift an entire company's mindset? Could they truly build a business that was not only profitable but also genuinely sustainable?

And most importantly—how many more lessons would they need before realizing that waiting for disasters to strike was no way to manage risks at all?

Risk Reduction and Resilience

Are You Reacting or Preventing? The Future of Risk Management

When it comes to risk management, many businesses operate under the false assumption that it's primarily about responding to crises. But this reactive approach can leave organizations dangerously exposed. To navigate tomorrow's turbulence effectively, companies must shift towards a proactive stance that anticipates and mitigates risks before they materialize. This shift is not just advisable; it's imperative for long-term resilience and success.

The first key lesson in this chapter is understanding the stark contrast between reactive and proactive risk management methodologies. Reactive risk management often leads to hasty decisions made under pressure, which can exacerbate problems rather than solve them. In contrast, proactive risk management involves identifying potential threats early and implementing measures to mitigate them before they escalate. This forward-thinking approach can prevent disruptions and reduce the overall impact of risks on the organization.

Consider a scenario where a company relies heavily on a single supplier for critical components. A reactive approach would involve scrambling for alternatives once the supplier fails, leading to production delays and financial losses. A proactive strategy, however, would involve diversifying suppliers long before any issues arise, ensuring continuity even in the face of unexpected disruptions.

The second lesson focuses on the importance of incorporating forward-looking strategies into business planning. Traditional risk management often overlooks long-term threats like climate change, technological shifts, and geopolitical instability. These emerging risks require an analytical lens that looks beyond immediate concerns to forecast future challenges. By integrating climate change projections into their strategic plans, companies can better prepare for regulatory changes, resource scarcity, and market shifts driven by environmental concerns.

Take the example of a coastal manufacturing plant at risk from rising sea levels. A reactive approach might involve dealing with flooding as it happens—an expensive and disruptive process. Conversely, a proactive approach would entail relocating operations or investing in flood defences well in advance, safeguarding the business against foreseeable threats.

Developing skills for identifying and mitigating emerging threats proactively is the third critical takeaway from this chapter. This involves cultivating an organizational culture that prioritizes continuous learning and vigilance. Employees at all levels should be encouraged to stay informed about industry trends and potential risks. Tools such as scenario planning, stress testing, and horizon scanning can help organizations visualize various futures and prepare accordingly.

In practice, this could mean regular training sessions on new regulations impacting your industry or workshops on technological advancements that could disrupt existing business models. Additionally, leveraging data analytics can provide deeper insights into patterns and trends that might indicate emerging risks. For instance, analysing social media trends could offer early warnings about reputational risks or shifts in consumer behaviour.

To solidify these concepts, real-life examples are invaluable. Consider how some leading companies have successfully navigated disruptions by being proactive: Netflix pivoted from DVD rentals to streaming services ahead of market demand; Tesla invested heavily in battery technology anticipating future energy needs; Patagonia champions sustainability anticipating consumer preference for ethical brands.

Ultimately, embracing proactive risk management isn't just about avoiding pitfalls; it's about positioning your organization for sustained success in an uncertain world. By adopting a mindset geared towards anticipation rather than reaction, businesses can enhance their resilience against disruptions while seizing opportunities that others may overlook.

In summary:

- **Contrast reactive vs proactive methodologies:** Understand why reacting is less effective than preventing.
- **Incorporate forward-looking strategies:** Plan with future risks like climate change in mind.
- **Identify and mitigate proactively:** Develop skills and tools to foresee and address potential threats.

Adopting these principles will not only protect your organization but also ensure it thrives amid tomorrow's uncertainties.

Contrast Between Reactive and Proactive Risk Management

Proactive risk management enhances resilience by embedding anticipation into the fabric of business operations.

The Importance of Forward-Looking Strategies in Business Planning

Incorporating forward-looking strategies into business planning is essential for sustainable success. This proactive approach allows businesses not just to survive but thrive by anticipating future trends and challenges. By integrating advanced analytics, scenario planning, and sustainability considerations into their strategies, businesses can pave the way for long-term viability.

Risk Reduction and Resilience

Forward-looking strategies involve understanding potential future scenarios that could impact the business environment. This includes everything from technological advancements, demographic shifts, climate change implications, to geopolitical trends. Businesses that adopt this approach are better equipped to adapt their operations proactively rather than reactively adjusting when it may be too late.

Consider the game of chess: a good player thinks several moves ahead, anticipating their opponent's actions and preparing countermeasures. Similarly, businesses must strategize multiple steps ahead in their industry landscape. They must foresee changes in consumer behaviour, regulatory shifts, or technological disruptions well in advance.

The integration of these strategies leads not only to resilience but also drives innovation within the company. Businesses begin viewing challenges as opportunities to innovate rather than obstacles that require firefighting.

How can your organization harness these forward-looking strategies? What tools and mindsets are needed to anticipate the future effectively?

Developing Skills for Proactive Threat Identification

To effectively manage risks proactively, developing certain skills is crucial. These include environmental scanning, trend analysis, and strategic foresight—skills that allow businesses to detect early signs of potential threats or changes in their operational landscape.

Training teams in these skills involves creating a mindset shift from reactive problem-solving to proactive opportunity-seeking. For example, regular training sessions can be held on how to use data analytics tools or how scenario planning works. Encouraging curiosity about external changes that could affect the company fosters an anticipatory culture.

A useful metaphor here is that of a sentinel standing guard—always watchful for signs of change or disturbance that could signal an approaching threat or opportunity. Just as sentinels protect their posts by observing patterns and anomalies, so too must businesses train their employees to monitor key indicators within their industry.

Implementing structured frameworks such as SWOT (Strengths, Weaknesses, Opportunities, Threats) analysis or PESTLE (Political, Economic, Social, Technological, Legal and Environmental) analysis helps organize this information systematically which aids in strategic decision-making.

By aligning these skills with sustainability goals, companies ensure that their growth does not come at an environmental or social cost but contributes positively towards global sustainability efforts.

Risk Reduction and Resilience

Ultimately, the transition to proactive risk management requires dedication but pays dividends in resilience and success. It empowers organizations to navigate tomorrow's turbulence with confidence and agility, ensuring they remain robust in the face of uncertainty.

Risk Reduction and Resilience

Reflections

1. How does our organization currently identify and prioritize potential risks, and what improvements can be made to our proactive risk management processes?

2. What strategies do we have in place to mitigate identified risks before they occur, and how do we measure their effectiveness?

3. How do we foster a culture of risk awareness and accountability across all levels of the organization?

4. What role does technology play in our proactive risk management efforts, and how can we leverage it more effectively?

5. How do we ensure continuous improvement in our risk management practices to adapt to evolving risks and industry changes?

Chapter 3: Extreme Weather Events

Learning Objective 1: Increasing frequency and severity of extreme weather.

Learning Objective 2: Failure to Mitigate Climate Change.

Learning Objective 3: Physical Damage to Assets.

The rain hammered against the window, a relentless symphony that blurred the cityscape outside. Sarah sat at her desk, fingers tapping absently on the oak surface. She glanced at the reports spread before her—pages filled with data on climate risks, mitigation strategies, and asset vulnerabilities. Her mind wandered back to last summer when a freak storm had flooded their main warehouse, causing millions in damages.

She remembered standing ankle-deep in water, feeling the cold seep into her bones as she surveyed the ruined inventory. The smell of damp cardboard and mould still lingered in her memory. They'd been unprepared then, caught off guard by nature's fury. Now, she vowed not to let it happen again.

Her eyes shifted to the window where raindrops raced each other down the glass. "We need to be proactive," she muttered under her breath. But how? The question gnawed at her like an itch she couldn't scratch. Implementing climate change adaptation strategies sounded good on paper, but translating that into actionable plans was another beast entirely.

A knock on the door pulled her from her thoughts. John entered, shaking off his umbrella and shrugging out of his wet coat. "Have you seen the latest forecast? Another storm's brewing," he said, dropping into a chair opposite her.

Sarah nodded, feeling a knot tighten in her stomach. "We can't afford another hit like last year," she said quietly.

John leaned forward, his face serious. "I've been thinking about our supply chain too," he said. "With these weather patterns becoming more unpredictable, we need to consider diversifying our suppliers."

She sighed and rubbed her temples. The weight of responsibility felt heavy today—a leaden burden pressing down on her shoulders. They needed more than just new suppliers; they needed a robust plan that encompassed every facet of their operations—from sourcing raw materials to ensuring employee safety during extreme weather events.

The room grew silent except for the rhythmic drumming of rain against glass. Sarah's mind wandered again—to dreams of a future where businesses not only survived but thrived by embracing sustainability wholeheartedly. Could they become pioneers in this movement? Could they set an example for others?

As she pondered these questions, she felt a flicker of hope amidst the uncertainty—a spark that urged her forward despite the challenges ahead.

What if embracing sustainability wasn't just about protecting assets but also about creating a better world for future generations?

Are You Prepared for the Next Big Storm?

The escalating prevalence of extreme weather events is a stark reminder of the pressing need to address climate change proactively. With hurricanes, wildfires, and floods becoming more frequent and severe, businesses face unprecedented challenges that threaten their assets and infrastructure. This chapter delves into the critical necessity for companies to integrate climate change adaptation strategies into their risk management frameworks. By doing so, they can bolster resilience against environmental risks while contributing to global sustainability efforts.

Extreme weather events are no longer anomalies; they are becoming the norm. Studies indicate a significant increase in the frequency and intensity of these events, driven largely by climate change. Rising global temperatures increase the amount of water vapour in the air. More water vapour in the air leads to more frequent and more intense rainstorms. For businesses, this means greater unpredictability and potential for disruption. The inability to predict and prepare for these changes can lead to catastrophic outcomes, including substantial physical damage to assets, operational downtime, and even long-term financial instability.

Ignoring climate change mitigation is not an option. The failure to address this issue will only exacerbate the problem, leading to even more severe weather patterns in the future. Companies that remain passive are not just risking their own futures but also contributing to a broader environmental crisis. It is imperative for businesses to take an active role in reducing their carbon footprint and implementing sustainable practices.

Physical damage from extreme weather can cripple businesses. Infrastructure such as buildings, transportation networks, and supply chains are particularly vulnerable. For instance, a single hurricane can cause billions of dollars in damage, disrupt supply chains for months, and lead to massive financial losses. Understanding these risks and taking steps to mitigate them is crucial for long-term resilience.

To navigate these turbulent times effectively, businesses must **assess their vulnerability** to extreme weather events. This involves conducting thorough evaluations of geographical locations, historical incidents, and the potential impacts on assets and operations. Identifying vulnerabilities allows organizations to prioritize areas that require immediate attention.

Next comes **identifying potential risks** associated with various types of extreme weather events—whether it's floods, hurricanes, wildfires, or droughts. Each type of event carries its own set of challenges and impacts, making it essential for businesses to consider both likelihood and severity when planning mitigation efforts.

Developing a robust contingency plan is another critical step. This plan should include measures such as strengthening infrastructure against extreme weather conditions, implementing early warning systems for timely alerts, and establishing clear evacuation protocols for employee safety. A well-crafted contingency plan can significantly reduce the adverse effects of extreme weather on business operations.

Steps must be taken to **enhance organizational resilience** beyond immediate mitigation efforts. This could involve investing in resilient infrastructure that can withstand harsh conditions, diversifying supply chains to reduce dependency on any single source or region prone to specific weather events, or setting up backup systems for critical operations to ensure continuity during crises.

Risk Reduction and Resilience

Proactive Steps: Building Resilience Against Extreme Weather

Assess Vulnerability

Start by conducting a thorough assessment of your organization's vulnerability to extreme weather events. Consider factors such as geographical location, past incidents, and the potential impact on your assets and operations.

Identify Potential Risks

Identify the potential risks associated with extreme weather events. This could include floods, hurricanes, wildfires, or droughts. Consider the likelihood and severity of each risk to prioritize your mitigation efforts.

Develop a Contingency Plan

Develop a detailed contingency plan to mitigate the impact of extreme weather events. This plan should include measures such as strengthening infrastructure, implementing early warning systems, and establishing evacuation protocols.

Enhance Resilience

Take steps to enhance your organization's resilience to extreme weather events. This could involve investing in resilient infrastructure, diversifying your supply chain, or implementing backup systems for critical operations.

Educate and Train Employees

Educate and train your employees on how to respond to extreme weather events. Provide them with knowledge and skills to ensure their safety and the continuity of operations during such events.

Test and Evaluate

Test your contingency plan regularly to ensure its effectiveness. Conduct drills and simulations to identify any gaps or areas for improvement. Evaluate the results and make necessary adjustments to enhance your organization's preparedness.

Monitor and Adapt

Continuously monitor weather patterns and stay updated on the latest forecasts and warnings. Stay vigilant and adapt your contingency plan as needed to address new risks and emerging trends.

Collaborate with Relevant Stakeholders

Collaborate with relevant stakeholders such as local authorities, emergency response teams, and other businesses in your area. Share information, resources, and best practices to enhance overall community resilience to extreme weather events.

Review and Update Regularly

Regularly review and update your contingency plan based on lessons learned from past incidents and changing risk landscapes. Stay proactive in managing extreme weather risks to ensure the long-term resilience of your organization.

By following these steps systematically—starting from assessing vulnerability all the way through regular reviews—you can create a resilient framework that not only protects your business but also contributes positively towards global sustainability efforts.

Increasing Frequency and Severity of Extreme Weather

Imagine a pot of water slowly coming to a boil. Initially, the changes are hardly noticeable, but as time progresses, the bubbles become more vigorous and frequent until they're rolling rapidly. This analogy mirrors how subtle climatic shifts have escalated into frequent and severe weather patterns that we can no longer ignore.

The economic impacts are profound. The Global Climate Risk Index 2021 pointed out that in the last 20 years, over 475,000 deaths were directly linked to more than 11,000 extreme weather events worldwide, with economic damages totalling around US$2.56

trillion. The increasing frequency of these events continues to strain resources and infrastructure, necessitating significant financial input for recovery and adaptation.

In regions where agriculture drives the economy, increased variability in weather conditions can lead to poor crop yields and higher food prices. Unpredictable weather patterns make it difficult for farmers to plan their planting and harvesting schedules, leading to inefficiencies and waste.

The shift towards more frequent and severe weather is undeniable and demands immediate action from all sectors of society.

Failure to Mitigate Climate Change

Physical Damage to Assets

Extreme weather does not discriminate – it impacts both small communities and global businesses alike. The physical damage to infrastructure caused by these events can lead to substantial financial losses for businesses, particularly those that are not prepared for such contingencies.

Think of it like this: a fortress may seem impregnable until a storm proves otherwise. Similarly, many businesses perceive their assets as secure until an unexpected natural disaster reveals vulnerabilities in their risk management strategies.

This section highlights the importance of resilient infrastructure. For instance, consider a manufacturing facility located near a flood-prone riverbank. Without proper defences such as elevated structures or flood barriers, one major storm could halt production indefinitely, leading to revenue losses and potentially jeopardizing customer relationships.

Developing resilience against extreme weather involves assessing potential threats specific to each location and business operation. Implementing robust materials and innovative construction techniques can be crucial in enhancing asset durability against natural disasters.

Integrating strategies that address increasing extreme weather frequency, mitigating climate change effects, and managing physical asset risks are essential steps towards building sustainable business practices that ensure long-term success.

These three focus areas – understanding changing weather patterns, acknowledging the risks of inaction on climate change, and protecting physical assets – form a triad of strategies that businesses must adopt for resilience in an era marked by environmental uncertainty.

Risk Reduction and Resilience

Consider the long-term benefits of these actions. Investing in renewable energy sources can reduce dependency on fossil fuels and lower operational costs over time. Implementing water conservation measures can safeguard against droughts that threaten production capabilities. Developing robust disaster recovery plans ensures quicker response times and minimizes downtime during extreme weather events.

In essence, embracing sustainability isn't just about mitigating risks; it's about seizing opportunities for innovation and growth. Businesses that lead with a genuine commitment to sustainability will find themselves better prepared for tomorrow's challenges while contributing to a healthier planet for future generations.

Key takeaways from this chapter emphasize the urgency of proactive climate action:

- **Increasing frequency and severity of extreme weather** necessitate immediate adaptation strategies.

- **Failure to mitigate climate change** poses severe risks to business operations and asset integrity.

- **Physical damage to assets** can be significantly reduced through resilient infrastructure investments.

Reflections

1. How prepared is our organization to handle the operational disruptions caused by extreme weather events, and what contingency plans do we have in place?

2. What measures are we taking to mitigate the financial impacts of extreme weather, including increased insurance costs and potential revenue losses?

3. How do we ensure the safety and well-being of our employees during extreme weather events, and what protocols are in place to protect them?

4. In what ways can we leverage technology and data to enhance our ability to predict and respond to extreme weather events?

5. How are we addressing the long-term strategic implications of climate change and extreme weather on our business model and sustainability efforts?

Chapter 4: Social Instability

Learning Objective 1: Operational Disruptions.

Learning Objective 2: Reduced Consumer Spending.

Learning Objective 3: Investment and Funding Challenges.

The sun dipped low over the horizon, casting long shadows across the cobblestone streets of Lisbon. The air carried the scent of salt from the nearby harbour, mingling with the aroma of freshly baked bread from a small bakery on Rua das Flores. Maria leaned against the counter of her family's café, her fingers tapping a restless rhythm. She gazed out at the dwindling crowd, her mind occupied by thoughts far removed from the picturesque evening.

Her father's voice echoed in her head: "You must always have a plan for when things go wrong." The old man had weathered many storms—economic downturns, supply chain failures, even political unrest. But this time felt different to Maria. The operational disruptions caused by recent global events had hit their small business hard. Suppliers delayed shipments or cancelled orders altogether. The regulars who once filled their tables now counted every euro before spending.

Risk Reduction and Resilience

Maria sighed and turned to wipe down an already clean table, her movements automatic and detached. She remembered how they had expanded their menu just last year, investing in new equipment and ingredients to attract tourists. Now those investments felt like anchors pulling them down into an uncertain future. Her thoughts drifted to Paulo, her younger brother, who had moved to Berlin for a job in tech. He had called last night with news that his startup was also struggling to secure funding.

A sudden gust of wind rattled the windows, snapping Maria back to reality. She glanced at the clock—nearly closing time—and began stacking chairs on tables with deliberate care. Each chair seemed heavier than usual as if burdened by her worries. Her mother entered from the kitchen carrying a tray of leftover pastries wrapped in cellophane.

"Take these to Senhora Almeida," she said softly, referring to their elderly neighbour who lived alone two blocks away.

Maria nodded and took the tray, feeling its warmth seep into her cold fingers. As she stepped outside into the cool evening air, she allowed herself a moment of quiet reflection. Could they adapt quickly enough? Would they find new ways to attract customers and secure supplies? Or were they merely delaying an inevitable decline?

She walked briskly through narrow alleys where street lamps flickered like weary sentinels guarding against encroaching darkness. Each step echoed with questions that demanded answers: How could they make their business more resilient? What contingency plans would safeguard not just their livelihoods but also those of their employees?

Arriving at Senhora Almeida's door, Maria knocked gently and waited until she heard shuffling footsteps inside. As she handed over the tray with a forced smile and exchanged pleasantries, another thought gnawed at her resolve—how many more times could they afford such small acts of kindness before it became unsustainable?

The night deepened as Maria made her way back home under a canopy of stars glinting like distant promises yet unfulfilled. She knew that solving these problems required more than just hard work; it needed foresight and adaptability woven into every decision they made.

But where would they begin this journey toward genuine sustainability?

How Operational Disruptions Can Ripple Through a Business Ecosystem

Understanding the impact of operational disruptions is not just about identifying immediate obstacles but also recognizing the profound, cascading effects these disruptions can have on various aspects of a business. When operations are interrupted, whether due to natural disasters, political instability, or supply chain issues, the entire business ecosystem can be affected. This chapter delves into the intricate web of consequences that follow such disruptions and emphasizes why robust contingency planning and adaptability are crucial for long-term resilience.

Firstly, let's define what we mean by *operational disruptions*. These are events that interrupt the normal flow of business activities. They can range from minor hiccups like temporary supply shortages to major crises such as cyber-attacks or geopolitical conflicts. Regardless of their scale, these disruptions often lead to significant operational setbacks. For instance, a factory shutdown due to unforeseen circumstances can halt production lines, delay shipments, and ultimately affect customer satisfaction and loyalty.

The immediate aftermath of operational disruptions often leads to **reduced consumer spending**. When businesses can't meet demand due to supply chain issues or production halts, consumers may turn to competitors or simply reduce their overall spending. This reduction in consumer activity doesn't just affect sales figures; it can have broader economic implications. Lower consumer spending can lead to a downturn in economic activity, affecting not only the business directly involved but also its partners and stakeholders.

Moreover, operational disruptions present serious **challenges for investment and funding**. Investors seek stability and predictability;

frequent disruptions undermine confidence in a company's ability to deliver consistent results. This can lead to reduced funding opportunities and higher borrowing costs. Companies facing operational challenges may find it difficult to attract new investments or maintain existing ones, which in turn hampers growth and innovation.

The interconnectedness of various business aspects means that an issue in one area can quickly spread to others. For example, a disruption in manufacturing might not only delay products but also increase operational costs due to expedited shipping needs or overtime pay for employees working extra hours to catch up on lost time. These increased costs can squeeze profit margins and limit available capital for other critical areas such as research and development or marketing.

Given these potential domino effects, it becomes clear why **contingency planning** is essential. Businesses need robust strategies in place to mitigate the impact of disruptions. This includes having alternative suppliers, flexible production capabilities, and comprehensive risk management plans. It's not just about having a plan B; it's about creating an adaptable framework that allows for swift responses to unexpected challenges.

Adaptability itself is another cornerstone for navigating these turbulent times. Businesses must be agile enough to pivot when

Risk Reduction and Resilience

necessary—whether that's shifting resources, changing suppliers, or even altering product lines temporarily to meet market demand. An adaptable organization is better equipped to handle short-term shocks without compromising long-term objectives.

Finally, **risk management strategies** must be ingrained into the corporate culture rather than being an afterthought. This involves continuous monitoring of potential risks, regular updates to contingency plans based on new data and trends, and fostering a culture where employees at all levels understand their roles in mitigating risks.

To summarize:

- **Operational Disruptions**: Events that interrupt normal business activities.

- **Reduced Consumer Spending**: A consequence of unmet demand leading consumers elsewhere.

- **Investment and Funding Challenges**: Loss of investor confidence due to instability.

By focusing on these areas through careful planning and adaptability, businesses can better prepare themselves for the inevitable uncertainties of tomorrow's turbulence while ensuring they remain sustainable both economically and environmentally.

Risk Reduction and Resilience

Operational Disruptions

Using technology effectively can also play a critical role in managing operational disruptions. Advanced analytics and real-time data monitoring can help predict potential issues before they become problematic. For instance, predictive maintenance on machinery can alert operators to possible breakdowns before they occur, thereby avoiding unexpected downtime.

Reduced Consumer Spending

When operational disruptions occur, one of the most immediate effects is often a reduction in consumer spending. This decline is primarily because disruptions typically lead to delays in production and service delivery, frustrating customers and eroding trust. For example, if an online retailer experiences a server outage during a high-traffic sales period, customers unable to complete their purchases may turn to competitors.

This drop in consumer confidence can have ripple effects throughout the economy. Reduced spending means less revenue for businesses, which may then need to cut costs by reducing staff hours or halting expansion plans. Each of these actions can further depress economic activity in a vicious cycle.

Why does consumer confidence wane during such times? It's largely about perception. If consumers feel uncertain about the stability of their favourite brands or the economy at large, they're more likely to tighten their belts as a precautionary measure.

To illustrate this with an analogy: consider consumer confidence as the fuel that powers the engine of the economy. When there's plenty of fuel (confidence), the engine runs smoothly with businesses thriving and expanding. However, when the fuel starts running low due to operational hiccups or broader economic troubles, everything begins to slow down - businesses must then find ways to reignite confidence and get things moving again.

Strategies businesses might employ include improving communication with customers about how issues are being resolved or offering guarantees and refunds where service has fallen short. These actions show commitment to customer satisfaction and help rebuild trust.

How then can businesses better prepare themselves for these eventualities? A key approach is diversifying supply chains and investing in robust IT systems that can handle increased loads or resist cyber threats effectively.

Could understanding and mitigating operational disruptions be the key to maintaining consumer spending during challenging times?

Risk Reduction and Resilience

Investment and Funding Challenges

Operational disruptions not only affect day-to-day business activities but also pose significant challenges for investment and funding opportunities. During periods of instability, investors tend to become cautious, pulling back from markets perceived as risky—which often includes companies struggling with frequent operational issues.

For startups or businesses seeking expansion funding during such times, this can mean delayed or denied funding rounds as venture capitalists opt for safer bets. Traditional lenders might also tighten their criteria for loan approval fearing defaults if business operations are not stable enough to ensure repayment.

To navigate these turbulent waters effectively requires businesses not only to manage current operations efficiently but also demonstrate resilience against potential future disruptions—essentially showing that they are 'disruption-proof' investments.

Consider this analogy: securing investment during uncertain times is like trying to build a house during a stormy season; you need solid foundations (stable operations) not just good blueprints (business plans). Without stability at its core—a foundation built on robust risk management strategies—a business will struggle to attract investment no matter how promising its potential might seem.

Risk Reduction and Resilience

A strategic approach here involves transparent communication with stakeholders about risk management practices in place—showing preparedness can reassure investors of your ability's resilience against operational hiccups.

Business leaders must think creatively about funding alternatives too; crowd-funding platforms or strategic partnerships might provide necessary capital when traditional routes are constricted by broader economic concerns or specific industry downturns.

Operational disruptions present significant challenges for investment and funding but overcoming these through strategic risk management enhances investor confidence and ensures financial stability—key components for sustainable success in any economic climate.

A genuinely sustainable business is not only environmentally conscious but also resilient against global supply chain disruptions, committed to workforce quality of life, and forward-thinking beyond mere growth metrics. These principles enhance long-term stability and foster trust among consumers and investors alike.

In practical terms:

- **Develop comprehensive contingency plans** that cover various scenarios.

- **Encourage a culture of adaptability** within your organization.

- **Implement robust risk management frameworks** to identify and mitigate potential threats.

- **Adopt sustainable practices** that ensure environmental stewardship, supply chain resilience, and workforce well-being.

Ultimately, navigating social instability requires a proactive approach that encompasses planning, adaptability, risk management, and sustainability. By focusing on these areas, businesses can better withstand the turbulence of tomorrow's uncertainties while ensuring resilience and long-term success.

Reflections

1. How does social instability in regions where we operate affect our supply chain and overall business continuity, and what strategies do we have in place to mitigate these risks?

2. What role does our organization play in contributing to or alleviating social instability, and how can we enhance our corporate social responsibility efforts to positively impact the communities we serve?

3. How do we monitor and respond to changes in social dynamics and public sentiment that could affect our brand reputation and stakeholder relationships?

4. What are the potential economic impacts of social unrest on our business, such as changes in consumer behaviour or disruptions in financial markets, and how do we prepare for these scenarios?

5. How do we engage with employees to ensure their safety and well-being during periods of social unrest, and what communication strategies do we employ to keep them informed and supported?

Chapter 5: Geoeconomic Confrontation

Learning Objective 1: Trade wars, economic sanctions.

Learning Objective 2: Involuntary Migration.

Learning Objective 3: Supply Chain Disruptions.

The afternoon sun cast long shadows through the office windows, creating a mosaic of light and dark on the polished wooden floor. David sat at his desk, fingers drumming a restless rhythm. The email from the cybersecurity firm still glowed on his screen, its words gnawing at him like termites in an old house. Another breach, this time targeting customer data. He leaned back in his chair, staring at the ceiling as if answers might be hidden among the cracks.

He remembered when he first started the company with high hopes and dreams of changing the world. Back then, everything seemed simpler. Now, every day felt like walking a tightrope over a pit of uncertainties. The recent trade wars had already strained their supply chain to its limits, and now this cyberattack threatened to unravel everything they had worked for.

A knock on the door interrupted his thoughts. Sarah stood there, her face a mask of concern and determination. "We need to talk about damage control," she said, stepping into the room. Her voice carried a weight that made David's chest tighten.

He nodded slowly, motioning for her to sit down. As she laid out their options—contacting customers directly, bolstering their cybersecurity measures—David's mind drifted to their last board meeting where economic sanctions had been a major topic of discussion. They had been cautious not to rely too heavily on any one market or supplier, but it seemed no amount of planning could shield them from geopolitical storms.

"David?" Sarah's voice pulled him back to the present.

"Sorry," he muttered, rubbing his temples. "It's just... we're juggling so many crises right now."

She sighed softly but offered a small smile. "I know it's overwhelming, but we have to focus on what we can control."

The room felt smaller with each passing moment as if closing in around them with invisible walls of pressure and expectation. David glanced out the window at the city skyline bathed in orange hues—a reminder that life moved forward regardless of their struggles.

"I've been thinking," he began slowly. "Maybe it's time we reevaluate our whole approach—not just patch up problems as they come but really rethink our sustainability."

Risk Reduction and Resilience

Sarah raised an eyebrow but didn't interrupt.

"We need more than just quick fixes," he continued. "We need long-term solutions that consider every aspect: environmental impact, supply chain resilience, workforce well-being... everything."

For a moment there was silence between them except for the distant hum of traffic below and faint chatter from other offices down the hall.

"You're right," Sarah finally said softly yet firmly. "But where do we start?"

David leaned forward across his desk; determination etched into every line on his face despite exhaustion tugging at him like an anchor pulling him down into murky depths.

"Let's start by asking ourselves what kind of future we're building—not just for us but for everyone involved with us."

Outside dusk began settling over buildings casting deepening shadows across streets bustling with life even amid uncertainty—a reminder that amidst chaos lay opportunities waiting patiently beneath surface turmoil.

What if true sustainability isn't just about surviving crises but thriving beyond them?

Risk Reduction and Resilience

The Silent Threat Lurking in Digital Shadows

In today's interconnected world, the rise in cyberattacks has become an undeniable reality that businesses must confront head-on. As we delve into Chapter 5, the focus shifts to the intricate dynamics of geoeconomic confrontation, where cybersecurity plays a pivotal role. A single breach can tarnish a company's reputation, erode customer trust, and inflict damage that extends far beyond immediate financial losses. This chapter underscores why businesses need to treat cybersecurity not merely as a technical concern but as a cornerstone of their brand integrity and long-term sustainability.

The backdrop of increasing trade wars and economic sanctions adds another layer of complexity to this scenario. These geopolitical tensions can exacerbate vulnerabilities, making companies prime targets for cyber espionage and attacks aimed at disrupting operations. When nations engage in economic warfare, businesses often find themselves caught in the crossfire, dealing with repercussions that ripple through their supply chains and market standings. This necessitates a robust cybersecurity framework that can withstand such external pressures while ensuring operational continuity.

Involuntary migration, driven by political instability or climate change, further complicates the picture. As populations move, so do

Risk Reduction and Resilience

talent pools and consumer bases. Businesses must adapt swiftly to these demographic shifts while safeguarding their digital infrastructure against threats that may arise from new and unfamiliar environments. Companies that fail to secure their data amidst such migrations risk not only losing critical information but also alienating their stakeholders who demand reliability and trustworthiness in uncertain times.

Supply chain disruptions, often triggered by geopolitical events or natural disasters, highlight another critical area where cybersecurity intersects with business resilience. A compromised supply chain can lead to delayed deliveries, product shortages, and significant financial losses. More importantly, it can damage a company's reputation irreparably if customers perceive that their personal data or transactions are unsafe. Hence, maintaining a secure and transparent supply chain is paramount for preserving customer trust and ensuring long-term success.

The Imperative of Cybersecurity in Modern Business

Cybersecurity is no longer just about protecting data; it's about maintaining a company's credibility in an era where digital interactions define customer relationships. **A breach can lead to immediate financial loss**, but the real damage often lies in the erosion of trust. Customers today are more informed and have higher expectations regarding how their data is handled. A single incident can lead to widespread distrust, prompting customers to seek alternatives who they believe offer better security.

Businesses must therefore adopt **proactive cybersecurity measures** rather than reactive ones. This includes regular vulnerability assessments, employee training on recognizing phishing attempts, and investing in advanced threat detection systems. By doing so, companies not only protect their assets but also demonstrate a commitment to safeguarding customer interests—an essential aspect of building lasting relationships in a digital age.

Trade Wars: A Catalyst for Cyber Threats

Trade wars and economic sanctions are increasingly common tools used by governments to assert dominance or achieve political goals. However, they come with unintended consequences for businesses operating globally. **Economic sanctions can isolate countries**, pushing them towards cyber warfare as a means of retaliation or survival. Companies must be vigilant about such risks by continuously monitoring geopolitical developments and adjusting their cybersecurity strategies accordingly.

Involuntary Migration: Adapting Amidst Change

The phenomenon of involuntary migration poses unique challenges for businesses seeking stability in turbulent times. As people migrate due to conflicts or environmental changes, companies must navigate new markets with diverse regulatory environments and potential cyber threats. Ensuring **data security across borders** becomes crucial as companies expand their footprint to accommodate shifting demographics.

Trade Wars and Economic Sanctions

Trade wars occur when countries impose tariffs or quotas on imports in an attempt to protect their domestic industries. The immediate effect is often an increase in the cost of goods, affecting both consumers and businesses. For instance, when Country A raises tariffs on steel imports from Country B, manufacturers in Country A may face higher costs for steel, potentially leading to increased prices for end products like cars and appliances.

Imagine a game of tug-of-war where each participant pulls harder in response to the other's force. This analogy mirrors the escalation seen in trade wars. As one country imposes tariffs, its trading partner might retaliate with its own tariffs, leading to a cycle of economic confrontation that can destabilize global trade patterns.

Economic sanctions, on the other hand, are penalties applied by one country or group of countries on another for various reasons, often political. These can include trade restrictions or financial constraints. Sanctions aim to pressure governments into changing policies without resorting to military action. However, while intended to target political elites, sanctions can also inadvertently harm ordinary citizens by limiting access to essential goods and services.

The impact of economic sanctions extends beyond immediate economic discomfort; it strains international relations and can lead to long-term diplomatic isolation. Countries under sanctions find themselves pushed towards economic desperation, often leading to political and social unrest.

In summary, both trade wars and economic sanctions disrupt global economic stability and have far-reaching effects on diplomatic relations and societal well-being.

Involuntary Migration

Involuntary migration is often sparked by conflicts, environmental disasters, or economic instability forcing individuals to leave their homes in search of safety or better opportunities. The United Nations Refugee Agency reports millions of involuntary migrants globally, highlighting the scale of this crisis. And this will increase as agricultural productivity decreases due to climate change and as NPK fertilizers becomes scarce.

Consider the plight of a farmer whose fields have been destroyed by floods—this person represents thousands who are compelled to migrate due to environmental catastrophes each year. Just as water flows from high ground to low during a flood, human populations move from zones of danger to perceived safety.

Countries receiving migrants are faced with challenges such as providing housing, healthcare, and employment. While some communities are welcoming, others might feel overwhelmed or threatened by the sudden demographic shifts, leading to social tensions.

Moreover, involuntary migration tests international solidarity as nations struggle with balancing national interests with humanitarian obligations. The rhetoric used in public discourse about migrants can influence societal attitudes significantly—ranging from empathy and support to hostility and xenophobia.

What if we viewed involuntary migration not as a burden but as a shared global responsibility? What insights might we gain about our collective humanity?

Supply Chain Disruptions

By understanding trade wars' impacts on global stability, recognizing involuntary migration's complexities as a shared responsibility, and mastering resilience against supply chain disruptions, businesses ensure not only their survival but also contribute positively toward global economic stability and ethical practices

Risk Reduction and Resilience

The complexities of geoeconomic confrontation present multifaceted challenges for businesses today. Trade wars and economic sanctions can disrupt market access and inflate operational costs. Involuntary migration, driven by political or environmental turmoil, can alter labour markets and consumer demographics. Supply chain disruptions—whether from natural disasters, political instability, or cyberattacks—can halt production and erode customer trust.

Key Takeaways

Businesses must adapt to these evolving threats by adopting a proactive stance. **Investing in cybersecurity** is no longer optional; it is a fundamental necessity. Not only does it safeguard data, but it also protects a company's reputation and maintains customer trust. In the digital age, a single breach can have far-reaching consequences, impacting brand integrity and long-term sustainability.

Moreover, companies must build **resilient supply chains** capable of withstanding geopolitical shocks. This involves diversifying suppliers, investing in local production where feasible, and maintaining strategic reserves of critical materials. By being agile and prepared, businesses can mitigate the risks associated with supply chain disruptions.

Risk Reduction and Resilience

Addressing the issue of **involuntary migration** requires a nuanced approach that considers both humanitarian aspects and business impacts. Companies should engage in ethical labour practices and support policies that stabilize affected regions. This not only contributes to global stability but also ensures a stable workforce.

Actionable Insights

1. **Prioritize Cybersecurity**: Implement robust cybersecurity measures to protect data and maintain trust.

2. **Diversify Supply Chains**: Reduce dependency on single suppliers or regions to enhance resilience.

3. **Ethical Labor Practices**: Support policies and practices that address the root causes of involuntary migration.

Reflections

1. How does geoeconomic confrontation impact our supply chain resilience, and what steps can we take to mitigate potential disruptions?

2. What are the potential financial implications of geoeconomic conflicts on our business, and how can we prepare for these scenarios?

3. How do we balance the need for market expansion with the risks posed by operating in geopolitically sensitive regions?

4. What role does our organization play in navigating regulatory changes driven by geoeconomic tensions, and how can we stay ahead of these developments?

5. How can we leverage emerging technologies and digital trade to mitigate the impact of geoeconomic confrontation on our operations?

Chapter 6: Cybersecurity Threats

Learning Objective 1: Increasing cyberattacks.

Learning Objective 2: Data Breaches and Loss of Sensitive Information.

Learning Objective 3: Damage to Brand Reputation and Customer Trust.

The coffee shop on the corner of Elm Street buzzed with the hum of conversation and the whir of espresso machines. Jack sat by the window, his laptop open but untouched. He stared out at the rain-soaked street, his mind tangled in thoughts about the recent data breach at his company. The incident had shaken him more than he cared to admit. His reflection in the glass showed a furrowed brow and eyes that had seen too many sleepless nights.

Jack's fingers drummed on the table as he replayed the events in his mind. The email from IT had arrived unexpectedly, a stark warning that sensitive customer information had been compromised. His first reaction was disbelief, quickly followed by a surge of panic. They prided themselves on their security measures—how had this happened? He took a deep breath, trying to calm himself.

A young barista approached with a steaming cup of coffee, breaking Jack's reverie. He nodded gratefully and took a sip, savouring the

Risk Reduction and Resilience

rich aroma and bitter taste that grounded him momentarily in reality. The room smelled faintly of roasted beans and rain-soaked earth, blending into an oddly comforting scent.

His thoughts drifted to their customers—people who trusted them with their personal information. Jack felt a pang of guilt as he imagined their reactions upon hearing about the breach. Trust was hard-earned and easily lost; how would they rebuild it? He remembered a conversation with his father years ago about running an honest business, one that valued integrity above all else.

Jack's phone buzzed on the table, displaying a message from his business partner, Laura: "We need to address this head-on." She was right; they couldn't afford to sweep this under the rug. Damage control was crucial now—not just for their reputation but for their own peace of mind.

As Jack pondered their next steps, he couldn't shake off another concern that gnawed at him: were they truly prepared for such cyber threats? And beyond immediate solutions, how could they ensure long-term sustainability in an ever-evolving digital landscape?

How can businesses fortify themselves against increasing cyberattacks while maintaining genuine trust and ethical responsibility towards their customers?

Risk Reduction and Resilience

Are You Prepared for the Cybersecurity Challenges of Tomorrow?

In today's interconnected world, the rise of artificial intelligence (AI) technologies has brought about significant advancements, but it also presents a myriad of cybersecurity threats. As businesses increasingly integrate AI into their operations, the ethical considerations surrounding its development and implementation become paramount. Ethical guidelines are not merely a theoretical construct; they are practical necessities to prevent adverse outcomes such as mismanagement, unintended consequences, and errors in AI systems. By prioritizing these guidelines, organizations can mitigate risks and ensure more responsible and sustainable use of this transformative technology.

The increasing frequency of cyberattacks is a stark reminder of the vulnerabilities inherent in our digital infrastructure. These attacks can range from data breaches to sophisticated hacking attempts aimed at disrupting services or stealing sensitive information. For businesses, the repercussions are severe: not only do they face financial losses, but they also risk damaging their brand reputation and losing customer trust. The ethical deployment of AI can play a crucial role in defending against these threats by promoting transparency, fairness, and accountability.

Risk Reduction and Resilience

Data breaches represent one of the most significant risks associated with cyberattacks. When sensitive information falls into the wrong hands, it can lead to identity theft, financial fraud, and other malicious activities. Organizations must therefore prioritize data protection by implementing robust security measures and adhering to ethical standards in AI development. This includes ensuring that AI systems are designed to protect user privacy and prevent unauthorized access to data.

The damage to brand reputation following a cybersecurity incident can be long-lasting and difficult to repair. Customers today are highly aware of privacy issues and expect companies to safeguard their personal information. A single breach can erode years of trust built with consumers. To maintain customer confidence, businesses must demonstrate their commitment to ethical practices by being transparent about how they use AI technologies and ensuring that these systems operate within established moral frameworks.

To effectively navigate these challenges, organizations need a structured approach to cybersecurity risk management. This involves assessing potential vulnerabilities, developing comprehensive strategies, implementing protective measures, and continuously monitoring for emerging threats. By embedding ethical considerations into each step of this process, companies can not only enhance their cybersecurity posture but also align their operations with broader societal values.

Risk Reduction and Resilience

In this chapter, we delve into a step-by-step process designed to help organizations fortify their defences against cybersecurity threats while upholding ethical standards in AI development and implementation. The goal is to provide actionable insights that will enable businesses to protect their assets, maintain customer trust, and contribute to a more secure digital environment.

The Comprehensive Cybersecurity Framework

Step 1: Assess Cybersecurity Risks

Begin with a thorough assessment of your organization's cybersecurity risks. Identify potential vulnerabilities by examining your IT systems, networks, and data infrastructure. This assessment should highlight areas where your organization may be susceptible to cyberattacks or data breaches.

Step 2: Develop a Cybersecurity Strategy

Based on your risk assessment findings, develop a cybersecurity strategy that outlines specific measures for protecting your organization's assets and data. This strategy should encompass both technical controls (like firewalls and encryption) and organizational controls (such as policies and employee training).

Step 3: Implement Protective Measures

Put in place protective measures to mitigate identified risks. This includes installing firewalls, encrypting sensitive data, using multi-factor authentication, regularly updating software, and training employees on best cybersecurity practices.

Step 4: Establish an Incident Response Plan

Create an incident response plan detailing procedures for detecting, containing, eradicating, and recovering from cyberattacks. Ensure that all employees understand their roles within this plan to enable swift action during an incident.

Step 5: Train Employees on Cybersecurity Awareness

Regularly train employees on cybersecurity awareness so they understand potential risks and recognize threats like phishing attempts. Educate them on best practices for using company systems securely.

Step 6: Regularly Test and Monitor

Continuously test and monitor your organization's cybersecurity measures through penetration tests, vulnerability scans, and security audits. Regular assessments help identify weaknesses before they can be exploited by attackers.

Step 7: Stay Updated on Emerging Threats

Stay informed about new cybersecurity threats by subscribing to industry newsletters or attending relevant conferences or webinars. Keeping abreast of trends helps you adapt your defences proactively.

Step 8: Establish Partnerships for Information Sharing

Form partnerships with other organizations for sharing information on cyber threats and best practices. Collaborate on threat intelligence sharing initiatives which can enhance collective resilience against attacks.

Step 9: Regularly Review and Update Cybersecurity Measures

Periodically review your cybersecurity measures considering technological advancements or lessons learned from past incidents. Adapting your defences ensures continued protection against evolving cyber risks.

By integrating ethical considerations into each step of this process framework—and maintaining flexibility—you foster an organizational culture that prioritizes security alongside responsibility towards societal values. This holistic approach not only safeguards against immediate threats but also builds long-term

Risk Reduction and Resilience

resilience essential for navigating tomorrow's turbulence successfully.

Increasing Cyberattacks

Cybersecurity threats are escalating, posing significant risks to businesses and consumers alike. In recent years, the frequency of cyberattacks has surged, with attackers becoming more sophisticated in their methods. This rise can be attributed to various factors including the increased digitization of assets and the widespread availability of hacking tools.

Think of the internet as a bustling city. Just as a city attracts more criminals as it grows, so does the digital world. The larger it gets, the more opportunities arise for malicious activities. Cyberattacks are like the digital equivalent of robberies and vandalism, disrupting lives and businesses.

It's important to understand that no sector is immune. From healthcare to finance, education to government agencies, all have witnessed an uptick in cyber incidents. These attacks not only cause immediate disruption but also long-term financial and reputational damage.

To put it into perspective, consider this: a single successful cyberattack can compromise thousands of personal records in mere minutes. The speed and stealth with which these attacks are carried out make them incredibly dangerous and difficult to counteract without proper security measures in place.

The key takeaway here is that the increasing complexity and frequency of cyberattacks necessitate stronger cybersecurity measures from both individuals and organizations.

Data Breaches and Loss of Sensitive Information

Data breaches have become alarmingly common, exposing sensitive information that can lead to severe consequences for individuals and companies. A data breach occurs when confidential information is accessed without authorization, often leading to identity theft, financial loss, and compromised personal safety.

Imagine if your home was left unlocked and someone walked in and stole your personal documents. A data breach is similar but on a much larger scale; it involves your digital home—where you store your most private information.

In recent times, high-profile data breaches have made headlines, affecting millions of users worldwide. Companies suffer not only immediate financial losses due to these breaches but also long-term damage to their credibility.

Why do these breaches keep happening? Often, they are due to inadequate security practices such as weak passwords, outdated

Risk Reduction and Resilience

software, or employee errors. Organizations must prioritize robust cybersecurity protocols to safeguard against these vulnerabilities.

Could understanding the nuances of these breaches help prevent them in the future?

Damage to Brand Reputation and Customer Trust

When a company suffers a cybersecurity incident, its reputation takes a direct hit. Customers begin to question the safety of their personal information and may hesitate to continue doing business with the affected organization.

Consider a bank that fails to protect its customer data; trust is the cornerstone of its relationship with customers. If that trust is broken, customers may very well choose to take their business elsewhere.

Cybersecurity Risk Management Framework

Identifying potential threats is the first step in our framework model. It involves scanning the digital environment to pinpoint vulnerabilities—much like checking all doors and windows in a house before leaving.

Next comes risk assessment—evaluating how likely it is for identified vulnerabilities to be exploited and what impact they would have if they were. This step prioritizes risks, helping organizations focus their resources effectively.

Mitigation strategies are then implemented; this could involve installing advanced encryption for data protection or conducting regular security training for employees. These actions are akin to installing better locks on the doors identified as weak points during risk assessment.

Finally, continuous monitoring ensures these measures remain effective over time. Regular audits help detect new vulnerabilities or attempts at intrusion early on before any significant damage occurs.

This proactive approach not only protects against immediate threats but also enhances long-term resilience by fostering a culture of security awareness among employees.

This framework ties together our learning objectives by showing how increased cyberattacks demand robust defences (objective one), how protecting data prevents breaches (objective two), and how safeguarding both fortifies brand reputation (objective three).

First and foremost, safeguarding sensitive information is not just a technical requirement but an ethical obligation. When organizations fail to protect customer data, they not only face financial repercussions but also damage their credibility and erode public trust. The ethical use of AI can mitigate these risks by ensuring that data handling practices are transparent, secure, and aligned with societal values.

Secondly, maintaining brand reputation hinges on trust and accountability. Ethical guidelines in AI development foster fairness and transparency, key components in building and maintaining customer loyalty. Organizations that prioritize ethical standards are better equipped to avoid public backlash and legal issues arising from mismanaged AI systems.

Lastly, adopting a proactive stance on cybersecurity demonstrates a commitment to long-term business resilience. As cyber threats evolve, so must the strategies to counteract them. Ethical considerations should guide these strategies to prevent unintended consequences that could harm both the business and its stakeholders.

Reflections

1. How comprehensive is our current cybersecurity strategy in addressing both existing and emerging threats, and what areas need improvement?

2. What steps are we taking to foster a culture of cybersecurity awareness across all levels of the organization, and how do we measure its impact?

3. How do we balance the investment in cybersecurity technology with the need for regular employee training and education to mitigate human-related risks?

4. What protocols do we have in place for responding to a cybersecurity incident, and how often do we test and update these protocols to ensure readiness?

5. How do we ensure compliance with relevant cybersecurity regulations and standards, and what are the consequences of non-compliance for our organization?

Chapter 7: Adverse Outcomes of Artificial Intelligence

Learning Objective 1: Mismanagement of AI technologies.

Learning Objective 2: Unintended Consequences and Errors.

Learning Objective 3: Ethical and Legal Issues.

The morning sun filtered through the blinds, casting slanted lines across the room. Sarah sat at her desk, her laptop humming quietly. She rubbed her temples, thinking about the quarterly financial report she had just reviewed. Rising costs had eaten into their profit margins again, and it felt like every month brought a new expense. Rent had gone up, utility bills were higher, and even basic supplies seemed to cost more than ever before.

She sighed deeply and took a sip of her coffee, now lukewarm but still comforting. Her mind wandered back to when she first started her small marketing firm five years ago. Back then, everything felt possible. The excitement of landing their first big client still played vividly in her memory. But now, with inflation running rampant and operational costs skyrocketing, it seemed as though they were constantly fighting an uphill battle.

Risk Reduction and Resilience

Outside the window, traffic hummed along the busy street below. The city was alive with its usual hustle and bustle; people hurried to work, vendors opened their stalls, and children laughed on their way to school. Sarah envied them for a moment—their lives appeared so simple compared to the complexities of running a business in these trying times.

Her phone buzzed on the desk beside her—an email notification from Mark, her CFO. "We need to discuss our cost-saving measures," it read. She knew what that meant: more difficult decisions about where to cut back without sacrificing quality or employee satisfaction. Sarah clicked open a spreadsheet that outlined various potential cuts—everything from reducing office space to renegotiating supplier contracts.

As she scrolled through the numbers, she thought about her team—their faces flashed in her mind one by one: Maria with her infectious laugh, Tom who always stayed late to finish projects on time, and Jenna who had just returned from maternity leave. How could she balance financial prudence with maintaining a supportive work environment?

A knock on the door interrupted her thoughts. It was Emily from HR holding a stack of papers—probably employee feedback forms on recent policy changes aimed at saving money.

"Got a minute?" Emily asked.

"Sure," Sarah replied, pushing aside the spreadsheet.

Emily handed over the forms and sat down across from Sarah's desk. "Some interesting feedback here," she said cautiously.

Sarah leafed through them quickly—comments about longer hours due to reduced staffing levels, concerns over health benefits being scaled back—all valid points that made this balancing act even more precarious.

She looked up at Emily and forced a smile. "Thanks for bringing these in."

Emily nodded sympathetically before leaving Sarah alone with her thoughts once more.

As midday approached and sunlight streamed brighter into the room—a stark contrast against Sarah's growing concerns—she wondered how much longer they could continue like this without making some drastic changes? How would they navigate this relentless tide of rising costs while staying true to their core values of sustainability and employee well-being?

What Could Go Wrong with AI?

Artificial Intelligence (AI) has undoubtedly revolutionized various industries, promising efficiency and innovation. However, recognizing and adapting to its potential adverse outcomes is crucial for businesses to remain sustainable. As we navigate an era of rising living costs and operational expenses, understanding the risks associated with AI can help companies avoid financial pitfalls and ensure long-term success. This chapter delves into the mismanagement of AI technologies, unintended consequences and errors, and the ethical and legal issues that businesses must consider.

Mismanagement of AI technologies is a significant concern. While AI can streamline operations and reduce costs, improper implementation can lead to inefficiencies and increased expenses. For example, an over-reliance on AI without proper human oversight can result in costly errors or system failures. Companies must invest in training employees to work alongside AI systems effectively, ensuring that both human intelligence and artificial intelligence complement each other. Furthermore, it's essential to regularly update and maintain AI systems to prevent obsolescence and security vulnerabilities.

Another critical aspect is **unintended consequences and errors** arising from AI deployment. Algorithms can sometimes produce biased or inaccurate results due to flawed data inputs or inherent design flaws. These errors can have far-reaching implications, from damaging a company's reputation to incurring legal liabilities. For instance, an AI system used for hiring might inadvertently discriminate against certain groups if not properly audited for bias.

Risk Reduction and Resilience

Businesses must implement robust testing protocols and continuously monitor AI outputs to identify and rectify such issues promptly.

The **ethical and legal issues** surrounding AI are equally important. As AI systems become more integrated into business operations, questions about data privacy, consent, and transparency arise. Companies must navigate these complexities by adhering to stringent regulatory standards and fostering a culture of ethical responsibility. This includes being transparent about how AI is used in their operations and ensuring that customer data is handled with utmost care. Failure to comply with these standards can result in hefty fines and loss of consumer trust.

Understanding the impact of rising living costs on business sustainability also involves examining how AI affects operational expenses. While automation can reduce labour costs, it may also require substantial upfront investments in technology infrastructure. Moreover, as living costs increase, businesses might face higher wage demands from employees who need to keep up with inflation. Balancing these financial pressures requires a strategic approach that prioritizes both technological advancement and fair compensation for the workforce.

Businesses must proactively manage their finances by exploring **cost-saving measures** without compromising quality or employee

Risk Reduction and Resilience

well-being. This might include optimizing supply chains through predictive analytics or adopting energy-efficient technologies to reduce utility expenses. By focusing on financial resilience and efficiency, companies can better withstand economic fluctuations and maintain their competitive edge.

In this rapidly evolving landscape, staying ahead of financial challenges necessitates a commitment to continuous learning and adaptation. Companies should foster a culture of innovation where employees are encouraged to develop new skills that complement emerging technologies like AI. Additionally, forming strategic partnerships with tech firms or participating in industry consortiums can provide valuable insights into best practices for managing AI-driven transformations.

Ultimately, embracing a holistic approach that considers environmental consciousness, global supply chain tolerance, workforce quality of life, and a post-growth mentality will ensure genuine sustainability for businesses navigating tomorrow's turbulence. By recognizing the potential adverse outcomes of artificial intelligence and addressing them proactively, companies can create robust frameworks that support long-term success amidst rising living costs and operational challenges.

In summary:

1. **Mismanagement of AI technologies**: Ensure proper implementation with human oversight.

2. **Unintended consequences and errors**: Regularly audit algorithms for bias and inaccuracies.

3. **Ethical and legal issues**: Adhere to regulatory standards on data privacy, consent, and transparency.

By focusing on these areas, businesses can mitigate risks associated with AI while fostering resilience against financial pressures brought about by increasing living costs.

Mismanagement of AI Technologies

The mismanagement of artificial intelligence (AI) technologies can be likened to a novice gardener attempting to prune a complex, sprawling vine. Without understanding the vine's growth patterns, the gardener might cut off vital branches, stunting growth or even killing the plant. Similarly, when businesses mishandle AI technologies, they risk undermining their own operational integrity and sustainability.

Unintended Consequences and Errors

In the realm of artificial intelligence, unintended consequences can emerge like shadows at dusk—subtly and unexpectedly. These shadows can cloud decision-making processes and lead to errors that might ripple through an organization's operations. Understanding these potential pitfalls is crucial for mitigating risks associated with AI deployments.

For example, an AI system designed to optimize inventory might inadvertently lead to overstocking popular items while neglecting niche but necessary products. Such errors not only affect operational efficiency but can also strain customer relationships and financial stability. The key here is not just recognizing these errors but learning how to anticipate and rectify them before they escalate.

Furthermore, the integration of AI into critical decision-making processes requires rigorous testing under diverse conditions to ensure reliability. Errors often occur when AI systems encounter scenarios they weren't trained on or when they interpret data through a biased lens unintentionally incorporated during their training phase.

Employing AI without fully understanding its decision-making pathway can be akin to setting sail without knowing how to navigate: both scenarios can lead you off course. Ensuring transparency in how decisions are made by these systems helps in creating trust and reliability in their outcomes.

Could exploring these shadows more deeply help us prevent the errors before they emerge?

Ethical and Legal Issues

Navigating the ethical landscape of artificial intelligence is as crucial as it is complex. Like city planners who must balance both the architectural integrity and the community's well-being in their designs, businesses must ensure that their use of AI respects both legal boundaries and ethical norms.

One major concern involves privacy issues; mishandling personal data can lead not only to legal repercussions but also damage a company's reputation permanently. It's imperative for companies to establish robust data governance frameworks that comply with laws like GDPR in Europe or CCPA in California, which aim to protect individual privacy.

Moreover, the ethical deployment of AI extends beyond legal compliance; it encompasses fairness and non-discrimination in automated decisions. Businesses need to scrutinize their AI models regularly for biases that could lead to unethical outcomes such as racial discrimination or gender bias.

Another layer involves accountability—determining who is responsible when an AI system makes a flawed decision that leads to adverse outcomes. Establishing clear guidelines for accountability can help mitigate risks and reassure stakeholders about a company's commitment to ethical practices.

Risk Reduction and Resilience

By maintaining vigilance over ethical standards and legal requirements, businesses harness the benefits of artificial intelligence while fostering trust and sustainability within their operations.

These three aspects—management precision, anticipation of consequences, and adherence to ethical/legal standards—are foundational pillars supporting sustainable use of artificial intelligence in business environments striving for long-term success amidst evolving global challenges.

Understanding the adverse outcomes of artificial intelligence is not merely an academic exercise; it is a business imperative. Mismanagement of AI technologies, unintended consequences and errors, and ethical and legal issues are all areas that demand our attention. Addressing these points head-on can significantly impact the sustainability of any business.

In summary, addressing the mismanagement of AI technologies, mitigating unintended consequences, and navigating ethical and legal challenges are essential steps toward achieving business resilience. Proactive financial management informed by these insights will enable companies to adapt to rising living costs and operational expenses effectively. By doing so, they can safeguard their future while contributing positively to broader societal goals.

Reflections

1. What measures are we implementing to ensure that our AI systems are free from bias and discrimination, and how do we validate their fairness and ethical use?

2. How do we address the potential job displacement caused by AI automation, and what strategies are we using to support workforce transition and development?

3. What protocols do we have in place to safeguard against cybersecurity threats associated with AI systems, and how do we ensure data privacy and protection?

4. How do we ensure compliance with existing and emerging AI regulations, and what steps are we taking to align our AI practices with legal and ethical standards?

5. How are we managing the reputational risks associated with AI, and what strategies do we have in place to maintain trust with our stakeholders?

Chapter 8: Cost-of-Living Crisis

Learning Objective 1: Rising living costs.

Learning Objective 2: Increased Operational Costs.

Learning Objective 3: Increased Financial Strain and Bankruptcy Risk.

Sarah stood at the window, watching the city lights flicker like scattered stars. The hum of traffic below was a constant reminder of the world moving on, indifferent to her worries. She sipped her coffee, feeling its warmth spread through her chest, but it did little to calm her racing thoughts.

The rising living costs had become an insurmountable mountain. Rent had gone up again, groceries were more expensive, and even the utilities seemed to conspire against her. She thought back to when she first moved to this apartment—how hopeful she had been then. Fresh out of college with a degree in business management, she believed she could conquer anything. Now, she felt as though she was merely surviving.

Her phone buzzed on the kitchen counter, breaking her reverie. It was a message from Mark, her business partner. "We need to talk about the increased operational costs," it read. Sarah sighed and put down her coffee cup with a soft clink. The bakery they started two years ago was struggling. Flour prices had skyrocketed due to supply chain disruptions and labour costs were up because they refused to cut wages for their loyal employees.

She walked over to the small desk in the corner of her living room, cluttered with receipts and invoices that seemed never-ending. The scent of fresh bread still lingered on her clothes from that morning's shift at the bakery—a scent that usually brought comfort now felt like a reminder of their financial strain. They had always prided themselves on using organic ingredients and paying fair wages, but those principles were becoming harder to uphold.

As Sarah sat down and opened her laptop, she wondered if there was another way out of this mess without compromising their values. Bankruptcy loomed like a dark cloud on the horizon—a possibility she didn't want to entertain but couldn't ignore either. Her mind wandered back to those late-night conversations with Mark about their dreams for the bakery: creating a community hub where people could feel at home while enjoying wholesome food.

The doorbell rang unexpectedly; it was Mrs. Thompson from next door bringing over some homemade cookies as a thank-you for fixing her garden fence last week. The simple act of kindness brought tears to Sarah's eyes—reminding her why they started this journey in the first place: community and connection.

"Maybe we need more than just good intentions," Sarah thought as she closed the door behind Mrs. Thompson with a grateful smile. Could they find a way to be genuinely sustainable—balancing environmental consciousness with financial viability while ensuring their workforce's quality of life? And if so, what would that path look like amidst rising living costs and increasing operational expenses?

Are You Prepared for the Next Financial Storm?

The escalating cost-of-living crisis is a pressing challenge that businesses can no longer afford to ignore. Rising prices, increased operational costs, and the looming threat of financial strain are reshaping the landscape of risk management. In this chapter, we delve into why businesses must not only react to crises but also anticipate and prepare for future threats. Specifically, understanding the potential risks associated with infectious disease outbreaks can underscore the importance of proactive planning, resilient operations, and a strong focus on health and safety measures.

Rising living costs have a direct impact on both consumers and employees. As prices soar for essentials like food, housing, and healthcare, disposable income shrinks. This creates a ripple effect—consumers cut back on non-essential spending, which in turn affects business revenues. For employees, higher living costs may lead to demands for higher wages or additional benefits, putting further

Risk Reduction and Resilience

pressure on company budgets. Businesses that fail to anticipate these changes may find themselves struggling to maintain profitability and retain talent.

Anticipating future threats like infectious disease outbreaks is integral to building business resilience. The COVID-19 pandemic has highlighted how unprepared many organizations were for such a global health crisis. The key takeaway here is that **proactive health and safety measures** are not just about compliance but about ensuring long-term operational continuity. Regular health screenings, flexible work arrangements, and robust remote work infrastructure can significantly reduce disruptions during an outbreak.

Resilient operations extend beyond immediate health concerns. Businesses must also consider broader environmental sustainability practices as part of their risk management strategy. Implementing eco-friendly policies not only helps in reducing operational costs but also appeals to a growing segment of environmentally-conscious consumers. Sustainable practices ensure that businesses are not just surviving but thriving in a world increasingly aware of environmental impacts.

A post-growth mentality is essential for long-term success in today's volatile environment. Rather than focusing solely on expansion and profits, businesses should aim for genuine sustainability—balancing economic growth with environmental stewardship and social responsibility. This holistic approach ensures that companies remain adaptable and resilient amid various crises.

In essence, navigating tomorrow's turbulence requires a multifaceted approach to risk management that includes anticipating rising living costs, managing increased operational expenses effectively, and preparing for potential financial strains due to unforeseen crises like infectious disease outbreaks. By fostering resilient operations through sustainable practices and proactive planning, businesses can safeguard their long-term success amidst an ever-evolving global landscape.

Rising Living Costs

Understanding the ripple effects of rising living costs on consumer behaviour and business operations is crucial for developing effective risk management strategies.

Increased Operational Costs

With every step up in operational expenses—from utility bills to supplier charges—businesses feel as though they're climbing an ever-steepening hill. This metaphorical hill represents the ongoing struggle companies face in managing overheads without compromising quality or profitability.

Risk Reduction and Resilience

Operational costs encompass everything from leasing commercial space to procuring technology necessary for daily operations. The rise in these costs often outpaces general inflation rates, placing an additional burden on businesses. For instance, technology upgrades necessary for maintaining competitive advantage can require substantial investment.

Consider a scenario where a company must upgrade its machinery to meet new environmental standards. While beneficial for long-term sustainability and compliance, the initial outlay can be substantial. Without careful planning and analysis, such investments could jeopardize a company's financial stability.

The use of renewable energy sources as an alternative to traditional energy options presents both a challenge and an opportunity. Initially more expensive, renewable technologies like solar panels eventually lead to lower operational costs and align with global sustainability trends—a critical consideration for future-proofing businesses.

Effective cost management strategies are essential here. Businesses might consider adopting lean management techniques or renegotiating supplier contracts to keep operational costs in check without sacrificing quality or output.

How might companies balance short-term financial pressures with long-term investment needs?

Risk Reduction and Resilience

Increased Financial Strain and Bankruptcy Risk

The threat of increased financial strain is real as businesses navigate through higher operational costs and reduced consumer spending power. This strain can escalate into bankruptcy risk if not managed strategically.

Consider this: A vessel (the business) in turbulent waters (the market) must not only stay afloat but also ensure it is not taking on water faster than it can be bailed out. The 'water' here symbolizes financial obligations—including debts and operational costs—that can overwhelm a business if not controlled.

Bankruptcy does not occur overnight; it is typically the result of prolonged financial pressure that exhausts a company's ability to adapt and recover. Factors contributing to this risk include decreased cash flow, high leverage ratios, and rigid cost structures that leave little room for adjustment during economic downturns.

To mitigate these risks, businesses must focus on improving cash flow management, enhancing operational efficiency, and maintaining flexible cost structures that allow for rapid adjustment according to market conditions.

A practical approach involves rigorous monitoring of key performance indicators (KPIs) related to financial health such as debt-to-equity ratio, quick ratio (liquidity measurement), and profit margins among others.

By understanding the interconnected nature of rising living costs, increased operational expenses, and heightened financial strain leading potentially towards bankruptcy risk—businesses can better prepare themselves for navigating these turbulent waters with resilience and strategic foresight

As you reflect on these points, ask yourself: *Is my business prepared for future economic uncertainties?* Are we investing in practices that ensure long-term resilience? By addressing these questions head-on, you lay the groundwork for enduring success amidst any crisis.

In summary, businesses must transcend short-term fixes and embrace comprehensive risk management strategies that prioritize sustainability, adaptability, and proactive planning. This approach will not only help navigate current challenges but also secure a thriving future in an increasingly unpredictable world.

Reflections

1. What strategies can we implement to manage the impact of rising costs on our pricing and profitability?

2. How can we better understand and address the changing needs and preferences of our customers during the cost-of-living crisis?

3. What measures can we take to support our employees who may be struggling with the cost-of-living crisis?

4. How can we enhance our operational efficiency to mitigate the impacts of increased costs related to suppliers and energy?

5. What role can corporate social responsibility play in our response to the cost-of-living crisis to maintain our brand reputation?

Chapter 9: Infectious Disease Outbreaks

Learning Objective 1: Continued risks of pandemics and infectious diseases.

Learning Objective 2: Health and Safety Liabilities.

Learning Objective 3: Operational Disruptions.

The sun hung low in the sky, casting long shadows across the bustling city street. Mark stood at the corner, waiting for the light to change. His mind wandered back to the meeting he had just left, where his team had discussed the latest outbreak of a new infectious disease. The conversation replayed in his head like a broken record.

"How can we ensure our employees' safety while maintaining productivity?" Sarah had asked, her voice tinged with concern.

Mark's thoughts were interrupted by the sound of a street musician playing a mournful tune on a saxophone. The notes floated through the air, mingling with the scent of freshly baked bread from a nearby bakery. He took a deep breath, trying to clear his mind.

He remembered the early days of his career when everything seemed simpler. Back then, he didn't worry about pandemics or operational disruptions. But now, as CEO of a growing company, every decision

Risk Reduction and Resilience

felt like walking on thin ice. He knew that one misstep could lead to disaster.

As he crossed the street, Mark's phone buzzed in his pocket. It was a notification about another article spreading false information about their company's response to the health crisis. His jaw tightened as he read it. Mis- and disinformation were like weeds in a garden; if not dealt with quickly, they could choke out everything good they had built.

He turned into an alleyway shortcut to his office and glanced at his reflection in a shop window—tired eyes stared back at him. He thought about how much was riding on their ability to navigate these turbulent times: employees' livelihoods, customer trust, and their company's reputation.

The alley smelled faintly of damp concrete and old newspapers. As he walked past graffiti-covered walls and discarded cardboard boxes, Mark couldn't help but wonder if they were doing enough to protect their brand image from being tarnished by falsehoods.

Inside his office building, Mark rode the lift up to his floor, feeling each jolt and rumble beneath his feet like tiny earthquakes shaking loose more doubts from within him. Was there something they were missing? Some strategy or approach that could help them not just survive but thrive despite these challenges?

When he reached his desk, Mark found himself staring out the window at the city below—a sprawling testament to human resilience and ingenuity—and pondered what it would take for businesses everywhere to genuinely embrace sustainability in all its forms: environmental consciousness, robust global supply chains tolerant of disruptions, workforce quality of life improvements...

Could they truly shift towards a post-growth mentality without sacrificing everything they'd worked so hard to achieve?

Unravelling the Impact of Misinformation on Infectious Disease Outbreaks

In today's interconnected world, the spread of misinformation is a formidable challenge that can have far-reaching consequences. Businesses must understand how false information proliferates to safeguard their brand image and maintain consumer trust. **The stakes are high**: mis- and disinformation can lead to reputational damage and manipulation of consumer behaviour, jeopardizing an organization's resilience and long-term success. Critical thinking skills in the general public are sadly lacking and this means that those in control over social media and mainstream news outlets have immense and predominantly unregulated power to influence opinion.

Infectious disease outbreaks are a prime context where misinformation thrives. The COVID-19 pandemic demonstrated how quickly false information could spread, influencing public perceptions and behaviours in detrimental ways. For businesses, this means navigating not just the health risks but also the misinformation landscape that accompanies such crises. Understanding the **continued risks of pandemics and infectious diseases** is crucial for proactive risk management.

Health and safety liabilities are another critical concern for businesses during infectious disease outbreaks. Companies must ensure their work environments are safe and comply with health regulations to protect both employees and customers. Failure to do so can result in legal repercussions and tarnished reputations. Misinformation can complicate these efforts by spreading unfounded claims about a company's practices or the nature of the outbreak itself.

Operational disruptions caused by infectious disease outbreaks can cripple businesses if not managed effectively. Supply chains may falter, workforce availability can plummet, and consumer demand may fluctuate unpredictably. Misinformation exacerbates these issues by creating confusion and panic, leading to erratic consumer behaviour and strained supply chains.

Risk Reduction and Resilience

Being vigilant and proactive in combating misinformation is essential for mitigating these risks. **Businesses must adopt a multi-faceted approach**, combining accurate information dissemination with robust health protocols and contingency planning. A comprehensive pandemic preparedness plan is not just a good-to-have but a necessity in ensuring business continuity amid such turbulence.

Step-by-step Process for Managing Infectious Disease Risks

Infectious Disease Risk Management Blueprint

Purpose: To safeguard business operations against the multifaceted threats posed by infectious disease outbreaks through vigilant risk assessment, preparedness planning, and misinformation management.

Step 1: Identify Potential Infectious Disease Risks

- Conduct thorough research on potential infectious disease risks relevant to your organization.
- Consider geographic location, industry specifics, and employee demographics.
- Gather data from credible historically prescient sources.

Step 2: Assess Vulnerability and Impact

- Evaluate how susceptible your operations are to infectious diseases.

- Analyse employee health risks, supply chain dependencies, customer interactions, and regulatory requirements.

- Use risk assessment tools to quantify potential impacts on various aspects of your business.

Step 3: Develop a Pandemic Preparedness Plan

- Create a detailed plan outlining steps for managing an outbreak.

- Include protocols for employee health monitoring, hygiene standards, remote work options, and communication strategies.

- Ensure the plan is adaptable to different types of infectious diseases.

Step 4: Establish Business Continuity Measures

- Implement measures to maintain critical functions during an outbreak.

- Develop remote work capabilities, backup systems for key operations, and identify alternative suppliers.

Risk Reduction and Resilience

- Regularly test these measures to ensure they function effectively under pressure.

Step 5: Communicate and Educate Employees

- Keep employees informed about infectious disease risks and safety measures.

- Provide regular updates on health protocols, training on hygiene practices, and clear guidelines for reporting illnesses.

- Foster an environment of transparency to build trust within your workforce.

Step 6: Stay Informed and Follow Guidelines

- Continuously monitor updates from public health authorities.

- Adjust your preparedness plan based on new information or changes in guidelines.

- Stay agile in responding to evolving health threats.

Step 7: Collaborate with Health Authorities and Experts

- Engage lightly with local health authorities for guidance and support. Use your discretion, experience and wisdom.

- Share information with industry peers to strengthen community-wide efforts against outbreaks.

- Leverage expertise from unbiased medical professionals to refine your strategies.

- Emulate International best practices.

Step 8: Regularly Review and Update Preparedness Plan

- Periodically review your pandemic preparedness plan based on past experiences and emerging risks.

- Update protocols as necessary to address new challenges or improve existing measures.

- Encourage feedback from employees to identify areas needing attention.

Step 9: Test and Evaluate Preparedness Measures

- Conduct simulations and drills to test your preparedness plan's effectiveness.

- Identify gaps or weaknesses through these exercises.

- Make necessary adjustments to enhance your organization's resilience against future outbreaks.

By following this structured approach, businesses can not only mitigate the direct impact of infectious disease outbreaks but also navigate the complex landscape of misinformation that accompanies such crises. The ultimate goal is to foster a genuinely sustainable business model that is environmentally conscious, resilient against global supply chain disruptions, committed to workforce well-being, and prepared for a future where adaptability is key.

Continued Risks of Pandemics and Infectious Diseases

The modern world, with its intricate tapestry of global connections, faces a persistent threat from pandemics and infectious diseases. As international travel and trade continue to expand, so too does the potential for rapid dissemination of pathogens. Recent history offers stark reminders, such as the COVID-19 pandemic, which demonstrated how quickly viruses can spread across continents.

Imagine our global transport network as a vast web spun by an industrious spider. Each thread represents connections between countries - air routes, shipping lanes, and land crossings. Just as a single tremor can send vibrations across the entire web, so too can a disease in one region quickly ripple across the globe. This analogy underscores the interconnectedness and vulnerability of our global system to health crises.

Despite advancements in medical technology and surveillance systems, several factors exacerbate the risk of future pandemics. Urbanization drives people into densely populated cities, ideal environments for viruses to thrive and mutate. Climate change also plays a role, affecting wildlife migration patterns and expanding the habitats of disease-carrying insects like mosquitoes.

Businesses are particularly affected by these outbreaks, facing disruptions that can range from minor delays to major halts in operations. The economic impact is profound; the World Bank estimates that a severe pandemic could cost the global economy up to $3 trillion. Companies must therefore prioritize robust contingency planning and health crisis management to safeguard their operations and workforce.

The omnipresent risk of infectious diseases continues to loom large, necessitating vigilant preparation and adaptive strategies from global businesses.

Health and Safety Liabilities

In the wake of any pandemic or widespread health crisis, businesses face significant legal and ethical responsibilities concerning the health and safety of their employees and customers. These obligations are not just moral but are also enshrined in various national and international laws. Companies must navigate these regulations carefully to avoid substantial liabilities.

Consider this: if a restaurant fails to adhere to health codes and a patron falls ill, the repercussions can be severe—not just legally but also in terms of public perception. Similarly, if a company neglects its duty to provide a safe working environment during an outbreak, it risks lawsuits, fines, and a tarnished reputation.

Risk Reduction and Resilience

The rhetorical question arises: How much is a business willing to invest now in preventative measures to save potentially exponential costs later? Proactive health policies and rigorous safety protocols are not merely regulatory compliance—they are crucial investments in a company's future stability and public trust.

Analogously, maintaining high standards for health and safety in business can be likened to installing both smoke detectors and fire extinguishers in every room of one's home after having fire-proof furnishings throughout (good diet and fitness regime). While the smoke detector provides early warning signs of danger (akin to monitoring systems for employee health), the fire extinguisher (comparable to emergency response plans) deals with crises effectively should they arise.

By fostering a culture that prioritizes wellness and safety above all else, companies not only comply with legal requirements but also enhance their brand loyalty among consumers who value corporate responsibility highly.

Could viewing health safety protocols as essential rather than optional lead businesses towards more sustainable practices?

Operational Disruptions

Operational disruptions during disease outbreaks present formidable challenges to businesses. The direct impacts include workforce shortages due to illness or quarantine measures, interruptions in supply chains due to logistic constraints, or mandatory closures enforced by government policies.

To visualize this impact effectively: imagine running a relay race where each runner represents a different segment of your company's operation—from production to delivery. If one runner trips or pauses—similarly if one part of your operation is halted—the entire race's pace is compromised until that runner regains momentum.

Factually speaking, during the 2020 pandemic-induced lockdowns, many businesses experienced firsthand how vulnerable their operations were to such unexpected halts. Retail sectors saw store closures while manufacturers faced delays due to broken supply chains; even digital services were strained by the sudden surge in online demand.

Adapting operational strategies has thus become paramount. Businesses must enhance their agility by diversifying supply chains or integrating flexible work models that allow them to respond swiftly to changing scenarios without compromising service delivery or employee welfare.

Moreover, lessons learned from past disruptions should guide future preparations—a concept akin to muscle memory where repeated practice helps an athlete perform better under pressure.

Risk Reduction and Resilience

Integrating resilience into business operations not only prepares companies for future disruptions but also aligns with broader goals towards sustainability and ethical responsibility.

By addressing these key areas—pandemic risks, health liabilities, and operational disruptions—businesses equip themselves against not only present challenges but also those yet unseen on our ever-volatile horizon.

The continued risks of pandemics and infectious diseases are a stark reminder that businesses must be prepared for the unexpected. **Health and safety liabilities** are not just regulatory requirements; they are critical to maintaining trust and operational continuity. **Operational disruptions** from outbreaks can cripple even the most resilient organizations if not adequately anticipated and managed.

Reflecting on these points, it becomes evident that businesses cannot afford to be complacent. The spread of misinformation can amplify the chaos during an outbreak, leading to reputational damage and consumer mistrust. To mitigate these risks, companies need a multifaceted approach:

- **Vigilance Against Misinformation:** Implementing robust communication strategies to counteract false information is essential. This includes monitoring social media, engaging with credible sources, and transparently communicating with stakeholders.

Risk Reduction and Resilience

- **Proactive Health Measures:** Regularly updating health protocols based on the latest scientific insights ensures that employee well-being is prioritized, which in turn sustains operational efficiency.

- **Contingency Planning:** Developing detailed contingency plans that account for various outbreak scenarios can significantly reduce operational downtime and financial losses.

Reflections

1. How prepared is our organization to respond to an infectious disease outbreak, and what are our current plans and protocols?

2. What measures have we put in place to ensure the health and safety of our employees during an infectious disease outbreak?

3. How do we effectively communicate with stakeholders (employees, customers, suppliers) about our response to infectious disease risks?

4. What contingency plans do we have for business continuity and operational resilience during an infectious disease outbreak?

5. How do we assess and mitigate potential financial impacts resulting from an infectious disease outbreak on our operations?

Chapter 10: Mis- and Disinformation

Learning Objective 1: The spread of false information.

Learning Objective 2: Reputation Damage.

Learning Objective 3: Consumer Behaviour Manipulation.

The sun dipped low over the horizon, casting long shadows across the narrow streets of Barcelona. Elena walked briskly, her mind a tangled web of thoughts. She had just left a meeting with her team, and the weight of their discussion clung to her like a damp mist. They had been talking about the recent spike in false information spreading about their company online—rumours that threatened to erode the reputation she had worked so hard to build.

Elena's heels clicked against the cobblestones as she navigated through the evening crowd. The scent of freshly baked bread wafted from a nearby bakery, momentarily distracting her from her worries. She remembered how her grandmother used to bake bread every Sunday, filling their home with warmth and comfort. But this was not a time for nostalgia; it was a time for action.

She glanced at her phone, which buzzed incessantly with notifications. Each ping felt like a jab, reminding her of the urgency

Risk Reduction and Resilience

of the situation. Elena knew that false information could spread like wildfire in today's digital age, and once trust was broken, it was nearly impossible to mend. She sighed deeply and turned into a quieter side street, seeking solace in the relative calm.

As she walked past an old bookshop, Elena's thoughts drifted to her competitors who seemed unaffected by such crises. Were they better prepared? Or did they simply have more resources at their disposal? Her own company had always prided itself on its sustainability efforts—using eco-friendly materials and ensuring fair wages for workers across their global supply chain—but now those very values seemed under threat.

Elena paused by a small park bench and sat down heavily. The cool metal seeped through her skirt, grounding her momentarily in reality. She looked up at the sky, now tinged with hues of orange and pink, and wondered if there was any way to turn this situation around without compromising their principles. Could they leverage technology better? Perhaps narrow the digital divide that seemed so insurmountable?

Her thoughts were interrupted by a group of children playing nearby, their laughter ringing out like bells in the evening air. Elena watched them for a moment before pulling out her phone again. She began drafting an email to her team—outlining strategies for countering

Risk Reduction and Resilience

false information while staying true to their mission of sustainability.

But even as she typed, doubts gnawed at her resolve. Was it enough? Could they truly navigate this storm without losing sight of what mattered most? And more importantly, how could they ensure that access to digital technologies remained equitable for all—so that no one else would have to face such challenges alone?

As Elena hit send on the email and stood up from the bench, one question lingered in her mind: In an era where misinformation can ruin reputations overnight and consumer behaviour is so easily manipulated by unseen forces—how do we create a future where businesses are not only sustainable but also resilient against such threats?

Are You Ready to Confront the Digital Divide?

In today's hyper-connected world, access to digital technologies is not just a matter of convenience; it's a fundamental determinant of opportunity and resource availability. The disparity in digital access has profound implications for individuals and businesses alike. When some have access to the latest tools and others do not, existing inequalities can widen, stifling innovation and economic growth. This chapter delves into the critical need to address these gaps, ensuring a more inclusive and sustainable business environment.

The rise of misinformation is one of the most pressing challenges exacerbated by unequal access to digital tools. False information can spread like wildfire, distorting public perception and decision-making processes. Businesses are not immune to this; a single misleading piece of information can wreak havoc on a company's reputation, affecting consumer trust and stakeholder confidence. Understanding how misinformation propagates and developing strategies to counter it is crucial for maintaining credibility in an increasingly sceptical world.

Greenwashing is the practice where companies make misleading or unsubstantiated claims about the environmental benefits of their products, services, or overall operations. This is done to appear more environmentally friendly than they actually are, often to capitalize on the growing consumer demand for sustainable and eco-friendly products. Greenwashing can involve using environmental imagery, vague terms like "eco-friendly," or emphasising minor green attributes to overshadow significant environmental harms. The general public is becoming more wary of eco claims due to several factors:

1. **Increased Awareness and Scepticism**: As environmental consciousness has grown, so has scepticism about corporate sustainability claims. Consumers are more informed and critical, often questioning the authenticity of green marketing efforts. A YouGov survey found that more than

half of global consumers are sceptical of brands' sustainability claims.

2. **Exposure to Greenwashing Practices**: High-profile cases of greenwashing have raised awareness about the practice. Consumers have become familiar with tactics like using misleading imagery or unverified certifications, making them more cautious when evaluating environmental claims.

3. **Demand for Transparency**: There is a growing demand for transparency and accountability from companies regarding their environmental impact. Consumers expect detailed, verifiable information about sustainability efforts, and are more likely to distrust companies that do not provide clear evidence of their claims.

4. **Regulatory and Media Attention**: Increased regulatory scrutiny and media coverage of greenwashing incidents have highlighted the issue, encouraging consumers to be more vigilant. Initiatives like the EU's Green Claims Directive aim to standardize and verify sustainability claims, adding pressure on companies to be truthful.

5. **Impact on Brand Trust**: Misinformation and deceptive practices have led to a loss of trust in brands that engage in greenwashing. Consumers are more likely to support companies that demonstrate genuine commitment to

sustainability, and they often share their scepticism with others, amplifying the demand for authenticity.

These factors contribute to a more discerning consumer base that is increasingly wary of eco claims, prompting businesses to adopt more transparent and genuine approaches to sustainability.

Reputation damage is another significant concern that stems from both misinformation and disinformation. Unlike misinformation, which may be spread unintentionally, disinformation is deliberately crafted to deceive. Companies must be vigilant in monitoring their digital footprint because even minor reputational hits can lead to severe long-term consequences. Proactive measures such as robust crisis management plans and transparent communication channels are essential for mitigating these risks.

Moreover, consumer behaviour manipulation through disinformation campaigns can lead businesses astray. With targeted falsehoods, unscrupulous entities can sway consumer opinions and choices, causing disruptions in market dynamics. Companies must invest in educating their customer base about recognizing reliable sources of information and encouraging scepticism towards dubious claims. A well-informed consumer is less likely to fall prey to manipulative tactics, fostering a healthier marketplace.

Access to digital tools also impacts how businesses can innovate and compete. Organizations with limited digital capabilities often find themselves at a disadvantage, unable to leverage data analytics, artificial intelligence, or other cutting-edge technologies that drive modern business success. This technological lag not only affects competitiveness but also limits the potential for sustainable practices that are increasingly demanded by consumers and regulators alike.

To narrow this gap, companies need to adopt a multifaceted approach that includes investing in digital infrastructure, providing training for employees at all levels, and advocating for policies that promote equal access to technology. By doing so, businesses not only enhance their own resilience but also contribute to a more equitable economic landscape where everyone has the opportunity to thrive.

Finally, fostering an inclusive business environment goes beyond mere compliance with regulations or meeting corporate social responsibility goals. It requires a genuine commitment to sustainability in all its forms—environmental stewardship, fair labour practices, and ethical governance. By levelling the playing field through improved digital access, companies can create a more balanced ecosystem where innovation flourishes without leaving anyone behind.

In summary:

- **Misinformation**: Understand how false information spreads and develop strategies to counteract it.

- **Reputation Damage**: Implement proactive measures like crisis management plans.

- **Consumer Behaviour Manipulation**: Educate consumers on recognizing credible information sources.

By addressing these areas head-on, businesses can better navigate the turbulence of tomorrow's digital landscape while fostering resilience and long-term success.

The Perils of False Information

In today's digital landscape, the spread of false information can occur at an alarming rate. Various platforms enable rapid dissemination of content, regardless of its accuracy. This phenomenon isn't just limited to social media; it pervades news websites, blogs, and even scholarly articles. The ease with which information spreads digitally means that falsehoods can travel just as quickly, if not faster, than the truth.

> *A lie can travel halfway around the world before the truth puts on its shoes.*
>
> *Often attributed to Mark Twain*

Imagine misinformation as a weed in a garden. Just as a single weed can quickly multiply if not managed, so too can a single piece of false information proliferate across digital networks, choking reliable sources and muddying the waters of discourse. This analogy helps us understand how misinformation can dominate and disrupt information ecosystems, often overshadowing the truth.

Research shows that once misinformation takes root, it is challenging to correct. People tend to hold onto first impressions or initial reports, even when presented with facts that contradict their beliefs. This cognitive bias complicates efforts to combat misinformation and necessitates sophisticated strategies to address its spread effectively.

Efforts to curb the dissemination of false information are multi-faceted. They involve fact-checking services, algorithms designed to reduce the visibility of identified false content, and educational programs aimed at improving digital literacy among internet users. These approaches are critical in helping individuals recognize and scrutinize the credibility of the information they encounter.

The key challenge lies in balancing freedom of expression with protections against harmful misinformation.

Understanding Reputation Damage

In a world increasingly driven by online interactions and transactions, an organization's reputation is its most valuable asset. Misinformation can severely damage this asset, leading to loss of consumer trust, declining sales, and potentially irreversible harm to

Risk Reduction and Resilience

brand image. The consequences can be particularly severe for businesses that fail to swiftly and effectively address false allegations or rumours.

Misinformation about a company can spread like wildfire. A single tweet or viral post containing inaccurate accusations or misleading facts about a product or service can result in significant reputational damage. Companies often find themselves in a reactive position, scrambling to mitigate the effects after the fact.

Consider this: if a brand is falsely accused of unethical practices, even if it manages to prove its innocence, the stain on its reputation might linger. This scenario is akin to trying to remove red wine from a white carpet; even if the stain fades, remnants often remain visible.

Businesses invest heavily in building trust with their consumers through years of consistent product quality and reliable service. However, this trust can be eroded in moments through the spread of misinformation. It's crucial for companies to not only protect themselves from potential falsehoods but also have robust crisis management strategies ready to deploy when needed.

Impact on Consumer Behaviour

Misinformation does not merely cloud public discourse; it has tangible effects on consumer behaviour as well. False information about products or health risks can lead consumers to make poor decisions that affect their safety and well-being. For instance, misleading claims about health supplements can lead people to use products that are ineffective or potentially harmful.

The manipulation of consumer behaviour through disinformation is akin to someone tampering with road signs leading travellers astray. Just as drivers depend on accurate signage for safe navigation, consumers rely on truthful information to make informed choices about what they purchase and consume.

By understanding these impacts—ranging from **the proliferation of false information** which seeds confusion much like weeds in a garden; **reputation damage** which threatens corporate integrity like an indelible stain; to **consumer behaviour manipulation** likened to deceptive signposts—it becomes clear how intertwined these challenges are with broader business sustainability goals focused on ethical operations and equitable growth opportunities.

Misinformation and disinformation can rapidly erode trust and credibility. In an age where digital access is ubiquitous, the speed at which false narratives can circulate is unprecedented. Organizations must invest in robust fact-checking mechanisms and maintain transparent communication channels to counteract these forces. It's not merely about damage control but about proactive engagement and education.

Reputation damage is often a byproduct of misinformation but can also stem from internal missteps or external attacks. The reputational capital of a business is a critical asset that demands constant nurturing. This involves not only addressing crises head-on but also building a resilient brand identity through consistent ethical practices and community engagement.

Consumer behaviour manipulation through misleading information can distort market dynamics and consumer trust. Businesses must strive to uphold ethical marketing practices, ensuring transparency in their communications and fostering an informed customer base. This approach not only mitigates risks but also builds long-term loyalty and trust.

Reflections

1. How does misinformation impact our brand's reputation and consumer trust, and what steps are we taking to proactively address these challenges?

2. What mechanisms do we have in place to monitor and respond to misinformation related to our products or industry, and how effective are these measures?

3. How can we enhance our media literacy and fact-checking processes to ensure that the information we disseminate is accurate and reliable?

4. In what ways can we engage with consumers to educate them about misinformation and encourage critical evaluation of the information they encounter?

5. What role does corporate social responsibility play in our approach to combating misinformation, and how can we align our efforts with broader societal goals?

Chapter 11: Digital Inequality

Learning Objective 1: The gap between those with access to digital technologies.

Learning Objective 2: Limited Market Reach.

Learning Objective 3: Operational Inefficiencies.

The sun had begun its descent, casting long shadows across the bustling streets of Nairobi. Aisha walked briskly, weaving through the crowd, her mind a whirlwind of thoughts. She felt the weight of her responsibilities pressing down on her shoulders like an iron yoke. The gap between those with access to digital technologies gnawed at her conscience. She had seen firsthand how it crippled potential and perpetuated inequality.

The scent of grilled maize filled the air, mingling with the exhaust fumes from idling matatus. Aisha's phone buzzed in her pocket, a reminder of yet another meeting. She glanced at the screen—an email from a rural community leader pleading for help to bring internet access to their school. Her heart sank. How could she bridge this chasm when resources were so limited?

Her thoughts drifted back to her childhood in Garissa, where she and her friends would gather under a baobab tree to study by the dim light of kerosene lamps. Those memories fuelled her determination but also reminded her of the long road ahead. The world had changed since then, yet some places seemed frozen in time, left behind by progress.

Aisha's pace slowed as she approached a small café where she often met potential partners for her initiatives. Inside, the clinking of cups and murmured conversations provided a momentary escape from her worries. She took a seat by the window and stared out at the street vendors setting up their stalls for the evening rush.

She couldn't ignore the operational inefficiencies that plagued many organizations attempting to address these issues. Resources were squandered on redundant processes while communities languished without basic necessities. Aisha tapped her fingers on the table rhythmically as she considered how best to streamline efforts and make every dollar count.

The waiter brought over a glass of water, its condensation leaving wet rings on the wooden table. Aisha sipped it slowly, lost in thought about environmental degradation caused by industrial activities nearby. How many more rivers would turn toxic before businesses embraced sustainable practices? The urgency was palpable; lives depended on it.

Her reverie was broken by the arrival of James, an old friend who now worked in renewable energy solutions. His presence was comforting but also brought fresh concerns to mind—how could they scale green technologies without exacerbating existing inequalities? They exchanged greetings and dove into conversation about possible collaborations.

As they spoke, Aisha felt a flicker of hope amidst her doubts and fears—perhaps there was a way forward after all. But one question lingered as they outlined plans: Could they truly create lasting change without compromising on sustainability and equity?

Discover the Unseen Divide: The Digital Inequality Challenge

The surge of industrial activities over recent decades has unmistakably shown how deeply intertwined human actions are with environmental consequences. Pollution, deforestation, and resource depletion have created a landscape where sustainable practices are no longer optional but essential. This chapter delves into the pressing need for businesses to adopt environmentally responsible strategies, emphasizing the importance of green technologies, reduced carbon footprints, and conservation efforts. By understanding the detrimental effects of industrial operations on ecosystems and communities, companies can play a pivotal role in fostering a sustainable future.

Digital inequality is an often-overlooked aspect of this broader environmental challenge. While digital technologies can drive efficiency and innovation, not everyone has equal access to these tools. **The gap between those with access to digital technologies and those without is a critical issue** that exacerbates economic disparities and limits opportunities for sustainable development. Businesses must recognize this divide and work towards bridging it by investing in inclusive digital infrastructure and education.

A significant consequence of digital inequality is **limited market reach**. Companies relying solely on advanced digital platforms may inadvertently exclude segments of the population who lack access to these technologies. This exclusion not only narrows the customer base but also stifles potential market growth and innovation. By adopting more inclusive strategies, businesses can tap into underserved markets, driving both economic growth and social equity.

Operational inefficiencies are another byproduct of digital inequality. Without widespread access to digital tools, many organizations struggle with outdated processes that hinder productivity and sustainability efforts. **Streamlining operations through technology** can lead to significant reductions in resource consumption and waste production. However, this requires a commitment to making these technologies accessible to all levels of the workforce.

Risk Reduction and Resilience

By addressing digital inequality head-on, companies can ensure they remain resilient amidst global challenges while fostering inclusive growth that benefits all stakeholders. The journey towards sustainability is complex but essential—embracing it fully will enable businesses to lead with purpose and integrity in today's dynamic landscape.

The Digital Divide: Access to Technology

The digital divide, a term first coined in the late 20th century, refers to the gap between individuals who have access to modern information and communication technology, and those who do not. This divide spans across geographic, socioeconomic, and demographic lines, affecting millions worldwide. In urban areas, high-speed internet and the latest devices seem ubiquitous, yet in many rural and low-income regions, such connectivity is a rare luxury.

Imagine a world where only one half of a town had electricity while the other did not. The side with power thrives at night under bright lights, their homes filled with warmth and the buzz of appliances. Across the street, darkness prevails post-sunset, activities limited to what daylight allows. This analogy mirrors today's digital divide: while some progress at high speed in education and business opportunities, others lag behind without these tools.

Statistics reveal that over 40% of households in lower-income countries still lack internet access. This gap is even more pronounced in less developed areas where infrastructure challenges persist. The implications are vast - from students unable to complete homework online to small businesses unable to tap into wider markets digitally.

The consequences extend beyond immediate inconvenience; they shape long-term societal structures. Without digital access, individuals miss out on educational content, healthcare information, remote work opportunities, and much more. Each of these elements is crucial for personal and professional development in today's global economy.

Access to digital technologies is not just about connectivity; it's about ensuring equal opportunities for all in a digitally-driven world.

Market Limitations Due to Digital Exclusivity

Limited market reach is another significant consequence of digital inequality. Businesses in digitally impoverished regions struggle to compete on a larger scale because they cannot engage with online markets effectively. This limitation not only hinders economic growth but also perpetuates regional inequalities.

Risk Reduction and Resilience

Why does this matter? Consider a local craftsman whose potential customers are primarily tourists visiting his small town. If his business were online, his artisanal products could reach an international audience year-round. Instead, his market is confined to those few who wander into his shop during tourist season.

This scenario highlights how digital tools can expand or limit economic opportunities. In 2019 alone, e-commerce sales surpassed $3.5 trillion globally, underscoring the vast potential of online markets. Yet businesses lacking digital capabilities miss out on this expansive marketplace.

The ripple effects are profound: communities remain economically stagnant as local businesses struggle to grow beyond physical boundaries. Additionally, consumers in these areas miss out on the benefits of global competition like lower prices and greater product variety.

Can you imagine how bridging this digital divide could transform economies and uplift entire communities?

Operational Inefficiencies Exacerbated by Digital Exclusion

The Digital Inclusion Strategy Framework

Operational inefficiencies are starkly evident in environments where digital technology is scarce or outdated. These inefficiencies manifest as slower communication channels, delayed processing times for transactions, and reduced productivity across sectors from healthcare to education.

Assessment Phase

The first component of our framework involves thorough assessment—identifying the extent of digital exclusion by evaluating internet penetration rates, assessing digital literacy levels among populations, and understanding economic barriers that hinder technology access. This initial phase sets the foundation for targeted interventions by highlighting specific needs within a community or organization.

Strategy Development Phase

Following assessment comes strategy development—tailoring initiatives that directly address identified barriers. For instance:

- Partnering with tech companies to enhance infrastructure.

Risk Reduction and Resilience

- Implementing training programs aimed at boosting digital skills.

- Lobbying for policies that make internet access more affordable.

Each initiative is designed with community-specific needs in mind to ensure relevance and effectiveness.

Monitoring & Evaluation

Lastly, monitoring and evaluating these initiatives are crucial for understanding their impact and adjusting strategies as needed. This ongoing process ensures that efforts remain aligned with goals and adapt to changing circumstances or new insights.

Interdependencies

These phases are interdependent; each feeds into the next creating a dynamic system that evolves over time. For example:

- Improved infrastructure increases internet usage statistics which in turn influences policy decisions.

- Enhanced skills lead to greater employability which boosts economic outcomes thereby providing further justification for investment in tech education programs.

Risk Reduction and Resilience

Practical Implications

For businesses adopting this framework means not just improving operational efficiency but also expanding market reach as more individuals gain online access thus broadening potential customer bases exponentially.

**This framework ties together key aspects of bridging the digital divide—accessibility literacy affordability—into a coherent strategy that can significantly enhance operational efficiencies while expanding market reach across previously underserved populations thereby contributing towards sustainable business practices globally."

The digital divide remains a critical issue that businesses must address to foster inclusive growth and operational efficiency. We have delved into the significance of access to digital technologies, the constraints on market reach, and the operational inefficiencies that arise from this inequality. These factors are not just technical challenges; they are integral to the broader goal of sustainability and responsible business practices.

So ask yourself: What steps can your organization take today to close the digital gap? Are there ways you can extend your market reach by fostering inclusivity? How can you optimize operations by ensuring equitable access to technology? Reflecting on these questions and taking actionable steps will not only mitigate risks but also position your business as a leader in sustainable and responsible growth.

By addressing digital inequality head-on, companies not only enhance their own prospects but also contribute positively to society at large. The path forward involves commitment and strategic action—ensuring that no one is left behind in our rapidly evolving digital landscape.

Reflections

1. How does digital inequality impact our organization's ability to reach and serve diverse customer segments, and what strategies can we implement to bridge this gap?

2. What role can our organization play in promoting digital literacy and access within the communities we operate, and how can this align with our corporate social responsibility goals?

3. How do we ensure that our digital products and services are accessible to individuals with varying levels of digital skills and resources?

4. What partnerships can we form with other organizations, governments, or NGOs to address digital inequality and expand digital access and skills training?

5. How can we measure the effectiveness of our efforts to address digital inequality, and what metrics should we use to track progress and outcomes?

Chapter 12: Human-Made Environmental Damage

> *Learning Objective 1: Industrial activities that cause pollution and environmental degradation.*
>
> *Learning Objective 2: Infectious Disease Spread.*
>
> *Learning Objective 3: Biodiversity Loss and Ecosystem Collapse.*

The sky had turned a bruised purple, the sun sinking below the horizon as Daniel walked through the industrial park. His boots crunched on gravel, and the air carried the faint scent of oil and metal, mingling with the distant hum of machinery. He glanced at his watch, feeling the weight of time pressing down on him. The board meeting was in two days, and he still hadn't figured out how to present his proposal.

He stopped by a chain-link fence, staring at the factory beyond it. This place had been his father's pride and joy—a symbol of progress and prosperity. But now, as Daniel looked at the plumes of smoke rising from its chimneys, he couldn't ignore the gnawing guilt in his stomach. Memories of summer afternoons spent playing near this very spot flooded back, but those days felt like another lifetime.

Risk Reduction and Resilience

His phone buzzed in his pocket. It was an email from Clara, his sustainability consultant. She'd sent over another report detailing the environmental impact of their operations. He skimmed through it: CO2 emissions up by 15%, water pollution levels dangerously high. The numbers blurred together, each one a testament to their complicity in degrading the planet.

Daniel sighed and leaned against a rusty lamppost. He remembered when Clara first joined them—young and idealistic, convinced that they could turn things around. Her passion had been infectious then; now it felt like a reminder of how far they still had to go.

A sudden gust of wind whipped through the park, carrying with it a chill that made him shiver. He thought about his daughter Lily and her questions about climate change during dinner last night. How could he look her in the eyes and tell her that he was part of the problem? The world she would inherit depended on choices made today—choices he had yet to make.

As darkness enveloped him, Daniel's mind drifted to other board members who saw sustainability as nothing more than a marketing gimmick or regulatory hurdle to clear with minimal effort. They didn't understand—or perhaps didn't want to understand—that true sustainability required more than just words on paper or token gestures.

The streetlights flickered on one by one, casting long shadows across the pavement. Daniel pushed himself off the lamppost and resumed walking toward his car parked at the edge of the carpark. His thoughts raced ahead: How could he convince them? What arguments would resonate?

He knew it wasn't just about saving face or meeting regulations—it was about survival itself. Businesses that failed to integrate sustainability into their core strategies risked becoming obsolete in an increasingly conscious world.

As he reached for his car door handle, another question gnawed at him: Could they truly transform their business model without sacrificing everything they'd built?

The Urgency of Sustainability Integration

Addressing human-made environmental damage is not just an ethical imperative; it is a business necessity. In today's rapidly evolving world, businesses face unparalleled challenges, from climate risks to societal expectations for sustainability. In this chapter, we delve into why integrating sustainability practices into business strategies is crucial for long-term risk mitigation and resilience.

Industrial activities are significant contributors to pollution and environmental degradation. Industries release pollutants into the air, water, and soil, affecting ecosystems and human health. For instance, manufacturing plants emit greenhouse gases that contribute to global warming. Likewise, chemical waste from factories often finds its way into rivers and oceans, disrupting aquatic life. It's essential for businesses to recognize these impacts and incorporate sustainable practices to minimize their environmental footprint.

Next, let's consider the **spread of infectious diseases**, a less obvious but equally critical aspect of environmental damage. Deforestation and habitat destruction force wildlife into closer contact with human populations, increasing the risk of zoonotic diseases like COVID-19. Urbanization and industrial agriculture exacerbate this problem by creating environments where pathogens can thrive. Businesses must adopt measures that promote environmental health to curb these risks.

Biodiversity loss and ecosystem collapse are other dire consequences of unsustainable practices. The extinction of species disrupts ecosystems that provide vital services such as pollination, water purification, and climate regulation. This loss threatens food security and increases vulnerability to natural disasters. Companies must support biodiversity through responsible sourcing and conservation efforts to ensure ecosystem resilience.

Risk Reduction and Resilience

Aligning Risk Management with ESG Factors

Incorporating Environmental, Social, and Governance (ESG) factors into risk management strategies is not merely about compliance; it's about aligning business operations with broader societal values. **Regulatory bodies worldwide are tightening standards on emissions, waste management, and resource use**, making it crucial for companies to stay ahead of these regulations to avoid penalties and reputational damage.

Moreover, **societal expectations are shifting towards greater corporate responsibility**. Consumers prefer brands that demonstrate a commitment to sustainability, influencing purchasing decisions and brand loyalty. Employees also seek employers who prioritize ethical practices and contribute positively to society. By embedding ESG principles into their core strategies, businesses can meet these expectations while fostering a loyal customer base and motivated workforce.

Real-Life Examples: Sustainability in Action

Consider the success stories of companies like Patagonia or Unilever that have integrated sustainability into their business models. Patagonia's commitment to environmental stewardship has not only earned them customer loyalty but has also set a benchmark in the industry for sustainable practices. Similarly, Unilever's Sustainable

Living Plan aims to decouple growth from environmental impact while increasing social impact—demonstrating that profitability and sustainability can go hand in hand.

Actionable Insights for Businesses

To make this integration practical:

1. **Conduct thorough assessments of your environmental impact**: Identify areas where your operations contribute most significantly to pollution or resource depletion.

2. **Implement sustainable supply chain practices**: Ensure your suppliers adhere to environmentally friendly practices.

3. **Invest in renewable energy sources**: Transitioning away from fossil fuels reduces carbon footprints and supports global climate goals.

4. **Engage stakeholders in sustainability efforts**: Foster a culture where employees, customers, and partners are encouraged to participate in sustainable initiatives.

Summary

Businesses must adopt sustainability as a core strategy rather than an afterthought. By addressing industrial pollution, mitigating infectious disease spread through better environmental stewardship, and preserving biodiversity, companies can reduce long-term risks while meeting regulatory requirements and societal expectations. Embracing sustainability fosters resilience against future uncertainties—a key ingredient for navigating tomorrow's turbulence.

Incorporating these insights will help you build a robust framework for sustainable business practices that not only protect our planet but also ensure your company's long-term success in an ever-changing world.

Integrating strategies for pollution control with efforts to halt habitat destruction could be key in preserving Earth's biodiversity. This holistic approach would support sustainability not just environmentally but also economically by ensuring long-term viability for businesses that depend on natural resources.

Integrating sustainability into business strategies is no longer a choice but a necessity. The pressing issues of industrial pollution, infectious disease spread, and biodiversity loss highlight the urgency for businesses to adopt comprehensive risk management practices that prioritize environmental stewardship. By addressing these challenges head-on, companies can mitigate long-term risks and ensure their resilience in an increasingly volatile world.

Industrial activities have undeniably contributed to economic growth, yet their environmental toll is substantial. Pollution and degradation not only harm ecosystems but also pose significant health risks to communities. Companies must recognize that sustainable practices are essential for maintaining regulatory compliance and meeting societal expectations. This involves investing in cleaner technologies, reducing waste, and enhancing resource efficiency.

The **spread of infectious diseases** serves as a stark reminder of how interconnected our world has become. The COVID-19 pandemic underscored the vulnerabilities within global supply chains and highlighted the importance of robust health protocols. Businesses must adopt proactive measures to safeguard their operations against future outbreaks. This includes implementing stringent hygiene standards, fostering collaboration with public health authorities, and promoting employee wellness programs.

Biodiversity loss and ecosystem collapse present profound threats to the stability of our planet. Healthy ecosystems are crucial for sustaining life and supporting economic activities. Businesses have a critical role in conserving biodiversity through responsible sourcing, habitat restoration initiatives, and partnerships with environmental organizations. By prioritizing ecosystem health, companies can contribute to a sustainable future while enhancing their reputations.

Risk Reduction and Resilience

To navigate tomorrow's turbulence effectively, businesses must align their risk management strategies with Environmental, Social, and Governance (ESG) factors. This approach ensures that they not only comply with regulations but also fulfil their ethical responsibilities towards society and the environment. By integrating sustainability into their core operations, companies can build resilience against future shocks and secure long-term success.

Assessing climate risks is a fundamental aspect of this integration. Companies need to conduct thorough evaluations of how climate change could impact their operations and supply chains. Developing adaptive strategies will help mitigate potential disruptions and capitalize on emerging opportunities in green markets.

Moreover, embedding **sustainable business practices** fosters innovation and drives competitive advantage. Organizations that lead in sustainability often attract top talent, gain consumer trust, and enjoy stronger investor confidence. It's essential for businesses to move beyond short-term gains and adopt a post-growth mentality that values long-term prosperity over immediate profits.

Reflections

1. How does our organization's operational footprint contribute to environmental degradation, and what steps can we take to minimize this impact?

2. What strategies can we implement to transition towards more sustainable practices, and how do these align with our long-term business goals?

3. How do we engage with stakeholders, including employees, customers, and suppliers, to promote environmental responsibility and awareness?

4. What are the potential risks and opportunities associated with environmental regulations and policies, and how can we proactively adapt to these changes?

5. How do we measure and report our environmental performance, and what metrics should we use to track progress and demonstrate accountability?

Chapter 13: Natural Resource and Energy Crises

Learning Objective 1: Scarcity of Plant and Animal Resources.

Learning Objective 2: Scarcity of critical resources such as water, minerals, and energy.

Learning Objective 3: Regulatory and Compliance Challenges.

The factory buzzed with the low hum of machinery. Shafts of sunlight pierced through the dusty windows, casting long shadows on the concrete floor. Maria stood by her workstation, her hands moving methodically as she assembled parts for the latest batch of electronics. Her mind, however, was far from the repetitive task at hand.

She thought about last night's news report—a major competitor had been exposed for dumping toxic waste into a nearby river. The public outrage was swift and fierce, with consumers vowing to boycott their products. Maria couldn't shake off the image of dead fish floating on the murky water, a stark reminder of what could happen if her own company didn't take their environmental responsibilities seriously.

Risk Reduction and Resilience

As she tightened another screw, Maria's thoughts drifted to a recent board meeting where they discussed their dwindling water supply. The factory relied heavily on local groundwater, which had been steadily decreasing due to over-extraction and climate change. She remembered how Mr. Thompson, the operations manager, had dismissed her concerns about investing in more sustainable water management practices.

"Too expensive," he had said with a wave of his hand, as if brushing away an annoying fly. "We need to focus on cutting costs."

Maria felt a knot form in her stomach at the memory. She knew that ignoring these issues would only lead to greater problems down the line—regulatory fines, reputational damage, and loss of consumer trust. She couldn't help but wonder if Mr. Thompson realized just how interconnected these risks were.

A loud clang jolted her from her thoughts as a toolbox toppled over nearby. She glanced up to see Jake muttering under his breath as he picked up scattered tools. Jake was new but already seemed worn out by the relentless pace and lack of support from management.

"Hey," she called out softly, "you okay?"

Jake looked up and forced a smile that didn't reach his eyes. "Yeah, just another day in paradise."

Risk Reduction and Resilience

Maria nodded sympathetically before turning back to her work. She couldn't help but think about how their approach to risk management was flawed—treating each issue in isolation instead of seeing them as part of a larger web that could either strengthen or unravel their entire operation.

As she continued working, Maria resolved to bring up these concerns again at the next meeting despite knowing it might fall on deaf ears once more. But what choice did she have? Ignoring these challenges would only lead them further down a path fraught with vulnerabilities.

Could they afford not to change course?

Unveiling the Hidden Pitfalls in Resource Management

Effective risk management is an intricate dance that often stumbles due to misconceptions. When it comes to natural resources and energy crises, these misconceptions can be particularly damaging. Misunderstandings about how risks interconnect and the erroneous belief that risk management is solely reactive can lead to significant oversights. This chapter delves into these issues, emphasizing the need for a proactive and holistic approach to ensure business resilience and long-term success.

One of the most immediate impacts of poor risk management in the context of natural resources is **reputational damage and loss of**

consumer trust. In today's hyper-connected world, companies are under intense scrutiny. A single misstep in handling a resource crisis can lead to a public relations disaster, eroding consumer confidence. For example, a company that fails to manage its water usage responsibly during a drought may face backlash from both consumers and regulators. This underscores the importance of integrating reputational considerations into your risk management strategies.

The **scarcity of critical resources** such as water, minerals, and energy poses another formidable challenge. Companies often operate under the assumption that these resources will remain perpetually available at stable prices. However, this is far from reality. Scarcity can lead to increased costs and supply chain disruptions, which in turn affect production schedules and profitability. It is crucial for businesses to recognize these vulnerabilities and incorporate them into their strategic planning.

In addition to reputational damage and resource scarcity, businesses must also navigate **regulatory and compliance challenges**. Governments around the world are tightening regulations related to environmental sustainability and resource usage. Non-compliance can result in hefty fines and operational shutdowns, further exacerbating financial strain. Therefore, staying ahead of regulatory changes and ensuring compliance should be integral parts of your risk management framework.

Risk Reduction and Resilience

Practical Steps for Robust Resource Risk Management

1. **Integrate Energy Risk into Planning:** Make energy considerations a core component of your risk management strategy.

2. **Resource Scarcity Assessment:** Conduct regular assessments to identify potential scarcities in critical resources.

3. **Regulatory Compliance Monitoring:** Stay updated on regulatory changes and ensure your operations are compliant.

Real-Life Examples

Consider the case of a beverage company that faced severe backlash due to its excessive water consumption during a regional drought. The company's reputation took a hit, leading to decreased sales and strained community relations. On the flip side, another company implemented water-saving technologies proactively, earning praise for its sustainability efforts and strengthening consumer trust.

Similarly, a tech giant experienced disruptions when rare earth minerals became scarce due to geopolitical tensions. By failing to diversify their supply chain earlier, they faced production delays and increased costs—lessons that underscore the importance of proactive resource planning.

Risk Reduction and Resilience

Interdisciplinary Approaches

Adopting an interdisciplinary approach can enhance your risk management strategy significantly. For instance:

- **Environmental Science:** Understand ecological impacts.
- **Economics:** Gauge market fluctuations.
- **Sociology:** Assess community reactions.

By merging insights from various fields, you gain a more rounded perspective on potential risks.

Key Takeaways

- Misconceptions about risk management can lead to significant oversights.
- Proactive strategies are essential for effective risk management.
- Integrate reputational considerations into your planning.
- Assess resource scarcities regularly.
- Stay ahead of regulatory changes.

The key takeaway here is clear: managing resources responsibly is not just an environmental need but a crucial strategy for maintaining consumer trust and corporate longevity.

Risk Reduction and Resilience

Scarcity of Critical Resources

Scarcity is becoming an increasingly pressing issue in our global economy. Essential resources like water, timber, fertiliser, ores, minerals, rare earths and energy are depleting at alarming rates while demand continues to soar due to population growth and industrial expansion. This scarcity poses not only environmental challenges but also significant operational risks for businesses across all sectors.

Water scarcity exemplifies this crisis profoundly. It's not just about having less water; it's about what this means for industries that depend on water for manufacturing processes or agricultural businesses that need it for irrigation. The ripple effect of water shortages can disrupt supply chains, inflate costs, and halt production, jeopardizing business continuity.

Minerals are another critical resource under strain. They are vital components in everything from electronics to vehicles. As these resources dwindle, the competition intensifies, leading to geopolitical tensions and trade conflicts that can further destabilize supply chains.

Energy resources are equally fraught with challenges. The shift towards renewable energy sources is imperative but comes with its hurdles such as investment costs, technology dependencies, and infrastructural adaptations. This transition phase is delicate; any

Risk Reduction and Resilience

misstep can lead to both operational setbacks and public relations disasters.

Now consider a game of musical chairs to represent the market's competitive nature over these scarce resources. Each player (business) vies for a seat (resource) when the music stops (supply diminishes). Those unable to secure a seat face significant disadvantages, potentially getting pushed out of the market entirely.

What would happen if we viewed resource management not just as a compliance obligation but as a strategic lever for long-term growth?

Regulatory and Compliance Challenges

Navigating the maze of regulatory requirements is a daunting task for any business involved in natural resources or energy sectors. These regulations are not static; they evolve in response to technological advances, environmental impacts, and societal demands. Staying compliant requires constant vigilance and adaptability.

For instance, emissions regulations have tightened significantly over the past decade in many countries. Businesses that fail to meet these new standards risk hefty fines, legal challenges, and severe reputational damage—think of it as walking on thin ice where any misstep could lead you into cold waters.

Risk Reduction and Resilience

One effective way businesses manage these challenges is through robust compliance programs tailored to their operations' unique aspects. These programs must be comprehensive yet flexible enough to adapt as regulations change—a dynamic dance between structure and agility.

Navigating regulatory landscapes effectively while managing scarce resources responsibly builds consumer trust through demonstrated accountability—a crucial pillar supporting long-term business sustainability

The **scarcity of critical resources** such as water, minerals, and energy poses another formidable challenge. Businesses must adopt sustainable practices to manage these resources efficiently. This involves not only conserving what we have but also innovating new ways to reduce dependency on finite resources. Proactive resource management strategies can provide a competitive edge, ensuring that businesses remain resilient even as global supplies fluctuate.

Further complicating this landscape are the **regulatory and compliance challenges** associated with resource management. Adhering to evolving regulations requires a forward-thinking approach and a willingness to invest in compliance measures. Non-compliance can result in hefty fines, operational disruptions, and long-lasting damage to a company's reputation.

Risk Reduction and Resilience

Reflections

1. How does our reliance on finite natural resources and energy sources affect our long-term business sustainability, and what steps can we take to diversify our resource base?

2. What strategies can we implement to enhance our energy resilience and ensure business continuity in the face of energy supply disruptions?

3. How are we addressing the potential financial impacts of rising energy costs on our operations, and what measures can we take to mitigate these risks?

4. In what ways can we engage with stakeholders to promote sustainable practices and reduce the environmental impact of our resource consumption?

5. What role can innovation and technology play in helping us adapt to natural resource and energy challenges, and how can we leverage these tools to gain a competitive advantage?

Chapter 14: Debt Crises, Demographics and Economic Shocks

Learning Objective 1: High levels of debt in governments and businesses.

Learning Objective 2: Sudden economic disruptions.

Learning Objective 3: Asset Bubble Bursts.

Jasper sat in his cluttered office, the hum of fluorescent lights above mixing with the distant sounds of the city below. He stared at the spreadsheet on his laptop, numbers blurring together like a watercolour painting left in the rain. The company's debt had climbed higher than he anticipated, and he knew something had to give. His fingers tapped rhythmically on the desk, a subconscious metronome counting down to an inevitable decision.

He remembered when he first started this business ten years ago. Back then, it was just him and a dream that felt as tangible as the leather-bound notebook where he jotted down his ideas. Now, he had employees depending on him for their livelihoods and investors expecting returns. It wasn't just about him anymore; it was about everyone who had put their trust in him.

Risk Reduction and Resilience

A sudden gust of wind from an open window scattered papers across his desk. He sighed and began gathering them up, feeling each rough edge between his fingertips. As he did, memories of past financial crises flickered through his mind like scenes from an old film reel: the 2008 crash when businesses folded overnight, friends losing homes and dreams alike.

Jasper leaned back in his chair and closed his eyes for a moment. He could hear distant sirens wailing outside, a reminder that life moved on regardless of individual struggles. The idea of shifting from reactive to proactive strategies gnawed at him like an itch he couldn't scratch. Could they really anticipate every potential threat? Was there even such a thing as being truly prepared?

A knock on the door pulled him back to reality. It was Maria from accounting, holding another stack of reports that needed immediate attention. Her tired eyes met his briefly before she placed them on his desk with a soft thud and left without a word.

As Jasper skimmed through the latest figures, doubts crept into his mind like shadows at dusk. Was it possible for any business to be genuinely sustainable? Environmental consciousness seemed like a luxury when survival was at stake; global supply chains were fragile; workforce quality often took second place to profit margins.

The weight of these questions pressed down on him until it felt hard to breathe. How could they balance growth with sustainability? And if they couldn't find that balance, what did that mean for their future—and for everyone else who depended on them?

Could embracing proactive strategies truly fortify them against unforeseen economic disruptions or would they always be one step behind an unpredictable world?

Are You Ready for the Next Economic Shock?

In today's volatile global landscape, businesses cannot afford to merely react to crises as they arise. The need for a shift from reactive to proactive strategies in managing debt crises and economic shocks has never been more urgent. As we delve into this chapter, it is crucial to understand that this transition is not just a strategic choice but a necessity for survival and growth in an unpredictable world.

High levels of debt in governments and businesses are a ticking time bomb. The global financial system is intricately interconnected, meaning that debt issues in one region can have ripple effects worldwide. Governments and corporations alike have borrowed heavily to finance growth, leading to unprecedented levels of leverage. This chapter will explore how these high debt levels can exacerbate economic instability and why it is vital for businesses to monitor debt indicators continuously.

Sudden economic disruptions are another critical area of focus. Whether it's a geopolitical conflict, a natural disaster, or an unexpected regulatory change, these disruptions can derail even the most well-laid plans. By adopting **proactive risk management strategies**, businesses can better anticipate these shocks and implement countermeasures before they escalate into full-blown crises. This approach requires a robust framework for continuous monitoring and early warning systems.

Asset bubble bursts present yet another formidable challenge. The euphoric rise in asset prices often leads to unsustainable valuations, setting the stage for dramatic declines. History has shown us that these bubbles can have catastrophic consequences, wiping out significant wealth and destabilizing economies. Through this chapter, you'll gain insights into identifying early signs of asset bubbles and understanding their potential impact on your business.

High Levels of Debt in Governments and Businesses

High levels of debt, whether in the realm of governments or businesses, pose a significant risk to economic stability. When entities borrow extensively, they become vulnerable to fluctuations in interest rates, economic downturns, and investor sentiment. For instance, if a government accumulates substantial debt during periods of low interest rates, a sudden increase can drastically raise repayment costs and destabilize its fiscal position.

Debt is like overloading a boat; too much weight and the boat risks sinking under even minor turbulence. Similarly, when businesses and governments carry excessive debt, even small economic shifts can trigger disproportionate consequences. This analogy helps illustrate the precarious balance these entities must maintain to navigate through financial waters safely.

It is important to understand that not all debt is inherently bad. Strategic borrowing can fuel growth and development when managed wisely. However, the key lies in sustainability — debts should be within a capacity that can be serviced even under less favourable conditions. This means maintaining debt levels that won't jeopardize an entity's long-term stability for short-term gains.

The global financial crisis of 2008 serves as a stark reminder of what happens when debt levels are not kept in check. Many businesses collapsed under the weight of their borrowing, unable to refinance or repay their obligations when credit conditions tightened. Governments had to step in with bailouts and stimulus packages, further straining public finances.

Maintaining sustainable debt levels is crucial for long-term economic stability and resilience.

Sudden Economic Disruptions

Sudden economic disruptions are events that abruptly alter the economic landscape, often leading to widespread financial uncertainty. These disruptions can stem from various sources such as geopolitical conflicts, pandemics, or technological breakthroughs. Their suddenness and unpredictability make them particularly challenging to manage.

Imagine a calm sea where businesses operate smoothly sailing ships; suddenly, a storm (economic disruption) hits. The ships (businesses) that have prepared for rough weather by reinforcing their structures will likely withstand the storm better than those caught off-guard.

Historically, sudden disruptions have led to severe economic downturns. The COVID-19 pandemic is a recent example where economies around the globe were disrupted overnight. Industries such as travel and hospitality were hit hardest, facing unprecedented revenue declines due to lockdowns and travel bans.

Businesses must develop agility and robust contingency plans to manage these shocks effectively. This involves diversifying supply chains, investing in technology for remote operations, and maintaining healthy cash reserves. Such preparedness doesn't just mitigate risks but also provides businesses with a competitive edge in recovering post-disruption.

The role of digital transformation in enhancing business resilience cannot be overstated. Companies that had embraced digital operations before the pandemic were better positioned to adapt to new working conditions and changing consumer preferences.

Could recognizing and preparing for these sudden changes be the key to not just surviving but thriving in today's volatile economic environment?

Asset Bubble Bursts

Asset bubbles occur when the prices of assets like stocks, real estate, or commodities significantly overinflate due to excessive demand driven by optimistic speculation rather than underlying fundamentals. When these bubbles burst, they lead to sharp corrections in asset prices which can devastate economies and businesses unprepared for such shifts.

Some contemporary potential investment bubbles include:

1. **Artificial Intelligence (AI)**: Investor enthusiasm for AI stocks has driven markets to new highs, reminiscent of past bubbles like the dot-com era. There is concern that the rapid rise in AI-related equity prices may not be sustainable, with some analysts warning of a potential bubble due to speculative investments and high valuations.

2. **Commercial Real Estate**: While not universally considered a bubble, certain segments of the commercial real estate market, such as office spaces, face significant challenges. Factors like new energy efficiency standards and changing

work patterns post-pandemic could lead to a re-evaluation of property values, potentially deflating prices in some areas.

3. **GPU Semiconductors**: The graphical processor unit semiconductor sector, closely tied to the AI boom, has seen substantial investment and stock price increases. This surge is partly driven by the demand for AI hardware, but there are concerns about whether the growth is sustainable or indicative of a bubble.

4. **Obesity and Oncology Drugs**: These sectors have experienced significant investment and stock price growth, raising questions about whether the current valuations are justified or if they reflect speculative excess.

5. **Cryptocurrencies and Meme Stocks**: Although not new, these areas continue to exhibit characteristics of speculative bubbles, with prices often driven by social media hype and investor sentiment rather than fundamental value.

These potential bubbles highlight the importance of careful analysis and risk management in investment decisions, as market dynamics can shift rapidly.

Consider a balloon being inflated beyond its capacity; eventually, it reaches a point where it cannot hold any more air and bursts suddenly. Similarly, asset markets can only stretch so far on speculation before they snap back to reality, often with painful consequences for investors and the economy at large.

The dot-com bubble burst at the turn of the millennium is a prime example of how speculative excess can lead to widespread financial disaster. Investors poured money into internet companies with high valuations but little substantive revenue—when reality hit, market values crashed dramatically.

To safeguard against such scenarios, it is essential for investors and businesses alike to focus on fundamental value rather than speculative growth. This strategy involves careful analysis of asset values based on actual performance metrics rather than projected future gains which may never materialize.

For businesses specifically, diversification across different asset classes can help mitigate risks associated with any single market's volatility. Additionally, maintaining liquidity ensures that companies have enough cash on hand to handle unexpected market corrections without needing to liquidate assets at unfavourable prices.

By understanding high levels of debt in governments and businesses; preparing for sudden economic disruptions; and recognizing signs of asset bubble bursts; entities can adopt more proactive strategies ensuring sustainability through inevitable cycles of economic changes.

Shifting from reactive to proactive strategies is no longer a luxury; it is an imperative for businesses aiming to navigate the intricate landscape of global risks. In this chapter, we examined the severe repercussions of high debt levels, sudden economic disruptions, and asset bubble bursts. These factors are not isolated incidents but interconnected threats that demand a comprehensive approach to risk management.

The critical takeaway from our discussion is that **proactive risk management** involves more than just having contingency plans in place. It requires **continuous monitoring** and **early implementation of countermeasures**. By anticipating potential threats rather than merely responding to them, businesses can enhance their resilience and adaptability in the face of future uncertainties.

Integrating Key Themes

Throughout this book, we have emphasized the importance of building a **comprehensive and actionable framework** to identify, analyse, and mitigate global risks. This framework is not static; it must evolve as new threats emerge and old ones morph. The core problem we aimed to solve was the lack of such a framework, which often leaves businesses vulnerable to fragmented and fast-evolving risk information.

Risk Reduction and Resilience

By now, you should have a thorough understanding of the most significant global risks identified by the World Economic Forum's Global Risks Report 2024. From environmental challenges to geopolitical tensions, each chapter has provided **practical strategies** and tools designed to help you manage these risks effectively.

A Holistic Approach

A sustainable business is one that genuinely incorporates environmental consciousness, global supply chain tolerance, workforce quality of life, and a post-growth mentality into its core operations. This holistic approach ensures not only business resilience but also long-term success.

- **Environmental Consciousness:** Sustainable practices are not just ethical choices but strategic imperatives.

- **Global Supply Chain Tolerance:** Diversification and flexibility in supply chains are crucial for mitigating disruptions.

- **Workforce Quality of Life:** Investing in employee well-being translates to greater productivity and loyalty.

- **Post-Growth Mentality:** Shifting focus from relentless growth to sustainable development can lead to more stable long-term gains.

Practical Application

What practical steps can you take today? Start by conducting a thorough risk assessment tailored to your unique business environment. Use the tools and strategies outlined in this book to create a dynamic risk management plan that evolves with changing circumstances. Engage with diverse perspectives within your organization and beyond, fostering a culture that values adaptability and innovation.

Remember, the goal is not just to survive but to thrive in an increasingly uncertain world. By adopting a proactive mindset, you position your business not only to withstand shocks but also to seize opportunities that arise from them.

As we conclude our journey through these chapters, it's clear that mastering global risk management is essential for ensuring business resilience and long-term success. The future will always hold uncertainties; however, with the right strategies in place, those uncertainties become manageable challenges rather than insurmountable obstacles.

Thank you for embarking on this journey towards building a more resilient and sustainable future for your business. Let's navigate tomorrow's turbulence together with confidence and foresight.

Reflections

1. How does our organization's financial strategy account for the potential impacts of debt crises, and what measures are in place to ensure liquidity and financial stability during such events?

2. What demographic trends are most likely to impact our workforce and customer base, and how can we adapt our business strategies to align with these changes?

3. How do we assess and mitigate the risks associated with economic shocks, such as sudden changes in interest rates or currency fluctuations, on our business operations?

4. In what ways can we leverage technological advancements and innovation to address challenges posed by demographic changes and economic volatility?

5. How do we engage with stakeholders, including employees, investors, and customers, to communicate our strategies for navigating debt crises, demographic changes, and economic shocks?

Chapter 15: Risk Assessment Frameworks

Learning Objective 1: The ISO 31000 framework.

Learning Objective 2: The Sendai Framework.

Learning Objective 3: Threat Reduction Handbook by Ernie Hayden.

The ISO 31000 Framework

The ISO 31000 framework provides guidelines for risk management applicable to any organization, regardless of size or industry. It is designed to help organizations manage risk effectively and enhance resilience. Below is an outline of the key components of the ISO 31000 framework:

Principles

ISO 31000 is built on several core principles that guide effective risk management:

1. **Integrated**: Risk management should be an integral part of all organizational processes and decision-making.

2. **Structured and Comprehensive**: A systematic approach ensures efficiency and consistent results.

3. **Customized**: Risk management should be tailored to the organization's external and internal context.

4. **Inclusive**: Involvement of stakeholders ensures that risk management is relevant and up-to-date.

5. **Dynamic**: Risk management must be responsive to change and anticipate emerging risks.

6. **Best Available Information**: Decisions should be based on the best available data, acknowledging its limitations.

7. **Human and Cultural Factors**: Risk management is influenced by human behaviour and organizational culture.

8. **Continual Improvement**: Organizations should continuously improve their risk management practices.

Framework

The framework component of ISO 31000 outlines how to integrate risk management into an organization's overall management system:

1. **Leadership and Commitment**: Top management must align risk management with organizational strategy and culture.

2. **Integration**: Risk management should be embedded in all aspects of the organization.

3. **Design**: The framework should consider the organization's context, allocate resources, and establish communication channels.

4. **Implementation**: An implementation plan should be developed, identifying decision-makers and modifying processes as needed.

5. **Evaluation**: The framework's performance should be measured against its objectives, and its suitability should be assessed.

6. **Improvement**: The framework should be continually adapted to address changes and improve its effectiveness.

Process

The risk management process in ISO 31000 is iterative and designed to identify, analyse, and treat risks:

1. **Communication and Consultation**: Engage stakeholders to ensure that risk management is relevant and effective.

2. **Establishing the Context**: Define the external and internal parameters to be considered when managing risk.

3. **Risk Assessment**: Identify, analyse, and evaluate risks to understand their potential impact.

4. **Risk Treatment**: Develop and implement strategies to mitigate risks to acceptable levels.

5. **Monitoring and Review**: Continuously monitor and review the risk environment and the effectiveness of risk treatments.

6. **Recording and Reporting**: Document and report risk management activities and outcomes.

The ISO 31000 standard provides a comprehensive approach to risk management that can be adapted to suit the specific needs and context of any organization.

The Sendai Framework

The Sendai Framework for Disaster Risk Reduction 2015-2030 is a global agreement aimed at reducing and preventing disaster risks worldwide. Here's an outline of its key components:

Expected Outcome and Goal

The framework's expected outcome is the substantial reduction of disaster risk and losses in lives, livelihoods, health, and assets of people, businesses, communities, and countries. Its goal is to prevent new and reduce existing disaster risks through integrated measures that strengthen resilience.

Seven Global Targets

Risk Reduction and Resilience

1. Substantially reduce global disaster mortality by 2030
2. Substantially reduce the number of affected people globally by 2030
3. Reduce direct disaster economic loss in relation to global GDP by 2030
4. Substantially reduce disaster damage to critical infrastructure and disruption of basic services by 2030
5. Substantially increase the number of countries with national and local disaster risk reduction strategies by 2020
6. Substantially enhance international cooperation to developing countries by 2030
7. Substantially increase the availability of and access to multi-hazard early warning systems and disaster risk information by 2030

Four Priorities for Action

1. **Understanding disaster risk**: This involves comprehending all dimensions of vulnerability, capacity, exposure, hazard characteristics, and the environment.
2. **Strengthening disaster risk governance**: This priority emphasizes the importance of disaster risk governance at national, regional, and global levels to manage disaster risk reduction across all sectors.
3. **Investing in disaster risk reduction for resilience**: This includes public and private investment in structural and non-structural measures to enhance economic, social, health, and cultural resilience.
4. **Enhancing disaster preparedness**: This priority focuses on improving response capabilities and implementing the

Risk Reduction and Resilience

"Build Back Better" concept in recovery, rehabilitation, and reconstruction.

Guiding Principles

The framework is based on several guiding principles, including:

- Primary responsibility of states to prevent and reduce disaster risk
- Shared responsibility between central government and national authorities
- Protection of persons and their assets while promoting and protecting human rights
- Engagement from all of society
- Full engagement of all state institutions of an executive and legislative nature at national and local levels

Implementation

The Sendai Framework is implemented through a multi-hazard approach, addressing risks from natural, biological, and technological hazards. It recognizes the role of various stakeholders, including local governments, the private sector, and other partners. The framework also emphasizes the importance of leveraging migrants' knowledge and skills in disaster risk reduction efforts.

Critical Infrastructure Risk Assessment: The Definitive Threat Identification and Threat Reduction Handbook

The Definitive Threat Identification and Threat Reduction Handbook by Ernie Hayden is a comprehensive guide focused on assessing and mitigating risks to critical infrastructure. Here is an outline of the book's key elements:

Risk Reduction and Resilience

Overview

The book serves as a hands-on, step-by-step guide to understanding, prioritizing, and mitigating risks associated with critical infrastructure. It is designed to be useful for both junior and senior personnel, including consultants, plant managers, corporate risk managers, engineers, and students.

Key Components

- **Understanding Risk and Risk Management**: The book provides a foundational understanding of what constitutes critical infrastructure and the associated risks. It covers the principles of risk management and risk assessment.

- **Risk Assessment Process**: Ernie Hayden details the entire risk assessment process, from pre-assessment planning to the final report. This includes preparing for site assessments, conducting observations and inspections, and balancing risk assessment activities.

- **Risk Assessment Methodologies**: The book outlines various risk assessment methodologies, helping readers identify the most applicable one for specific assessments. It includes qualitative risk management practices and touches on quantitative practices related to cybersecurity.

- **Practical Examples and Tools**: The book includes a real-world example risk assessment report, providing practical lessons and guidance. It also offers tools and examples to help readers perform large-facility risk assessments.

- **Sample Risk Assessment Report**: An appendix in the book provides a sample risk assessment report, demonstrating the application of the lessons and guidance provided throughout the book.

Additional Features

- **International Perspective**: While the book is rooted in U.S. critical infrastructure, it also provides insights into risk assessment practices in other countries like Canada and the UK.
- **Comprehensive Coverage**: The book is over 400 pages long and includes detailed discussions on the tools and processes needed for performing physical risk assessments.
- **Target Audience**: The book is intended for a wide range of professionals involved in critical infrastructure, from seasoned managers to new employees, making it a valuable resource for anyone tasked with assessing and mitigating risks in this field.

Overall, Ernie Hayden's handbook is a detailed and practical guide for conducting risk assessments on critical infrastructure, providing essential knowledge and tools for security specialists and risk managers.

Choosing the appropriate risk management framework

Choosing the appropriate framework for your organization involves a thorough understanding of your specific needs, objectives, and risk profile. Here are the steps to guide you in selecting the most suitable framework:

1. Identify Organizational Needs

- **Assess Specific Requirements**: Understand the unique needs of your organization, including industry, size, complexity, and risk tolerance. Determine whether your primary concerns are financial risks, cybersecurity, compliance, or a combination of factors.

2. Evaluate Framework Options

- **Research Available Frameworks**: Familiarize yourself with various risk management frameworks such as ISO 31000, COSO ERM, NIST Cybersecurity Framework, and others. Each framework has its strengths and weaknesses, so thorough research and comparison are essential.

3. Consult with Stakeholders

- **Engage Key Personnel**: Involve senior management, risk managers, compliance officers, and IT professionals in the decision-making process. Their insights on priorities and concerns will be invaluable in selecting a framework that aligns with organizational goals.

4. Evaluate Framework Compatibility

- **Assess Alignment with Existing Processes**: Determine how well each framework integrates with your current processes and organizational culture. A framework that fits seamlessly is more likely to be successful.

5. Consider Scalability

- **Ensure Adaptability**: Choose a framework that can grow with your organization and adapt to new challenges. Scalability is crucial for maintaining effective risk management over time.

6. Training and Resources

- **Evaluate Training Availability**: Ensure that there are adequate training resources and expertise available for the chosen framework, enabling your team to implement it effectively.

7. Cost Analysis

- **Analyse Costs vs. Benefits**: Consider the cost of implementing and maintaining the framework, including software, training, and ongoing support. Compare these costs against the potential benefits and risk reduction.

8. Pilot Implementation

- **Test the Framework**: Before full-scale implementation, consider piloting the framework in a specific department or project to assess its effectiveness and feasibility.

9. Continuous Improvement

- **Regular Review and Update**: Understand that risk management is an ongoing process. Regularly review and update your framework to address emerging risks and changes in your organization.

Follow these steps to select a risk management framework that not only addresses your current needs but also supports your organization's growth and resilience in the face of future challenges.

Epilogue

Navigating the Future: A Conclusive Blueprint for Mastery in Global Risk Management

As we draw the curtains on this exploration of global risk management, it is crucial to reflect on the journey we have undertaken together. This book has aimed to arm you with the knowledge and tools necessary to navigate the increasingly turbulent waters of global business environments. From understanding the nuances of geopolitical tensions to mastering the intricacies of technological disruptions, we have covered a vast landscape of potential threats and opportunities.

Real-world applications of this book are vast and varied, reflecting the diverse backgrounds from which our readers come. Senior executives can leverage these insights to refine their strategic planning processes, ensuring that risk management is an integral part of their decision-making framework. Risk managers will find the detailed analysis and proposed frameworks invaluable in updating their current practices to meet emerging challenges head-on.

Risk Reduction and Resilience

To **recap**, here are the key takeaways:

- The importance of proactive risk identification and continuous monitoring.
- Strategies for building resilient organizational structures that can withstand global shocks.
- Techniques for fostering a culture that embraces change and uncertainty as opportunities for innovation.

Implementing these strategies requires more than just understanding; it necessitates action. Here are some recommendations:

1. **Integrate risk management** into all levels of strategic planning.
2. **Cultivate a robust internal culture** that values adaptability and foresight.
3. **Leverage technology** not just as a tool, but as a fundamental pillar of your risk management strategy.

However, it's important to acknowledge that no single book can cover all possible contingencies or predict every turn in the road. The fields of global risks are ever-evolving, and continuous education and adaptation are essential. Further research is needed in

Risk Reduction and Resilience

areas such as cyber security threats which continue to evolve at a rapid pace, and the impact of climate change on different industries.

I encourage you to not just read but act on the insights provided here. The real test of understanding comes from application in real-life scenarios—turn these strategies into everyday practices.

As we conclude, remember that managing risk isn't just about preventing losses; it's about creating opportunities for significant gains in stability, reputation, and operational efficiency. Let this book be a guide, but let your experiences lead you forward.

Be bold in your pursuit of resilience; let foresight be your guide, adaptability your tool, and wisdom your companion.

"The only way to make sense out of change is to plunge into it, move with it, and join the dance."

Alan Watts

This quote beautifully encapsulates our discussion: embracing change is not merely a necessity but an opportunity to lead and excel in an unpredictable world.

References

Risk Planning Manual

Critical Infrastructure Risk Assessment: The Definitive Threat Identification and Threat Reduction Handbook Kindle Edition by Ernie Hayden (Author). ISBN : 1944480714

Global Risk Reports

WEF The Global Risks Report 2024
www.weforum.org/publications/global-risks-report-2024.
ISBN: 978-2-940631-64-3

PwC Global Risks Report 2024
pwcplus.de/en/article/241394/global-risks-report-2024/

KPMG Climate Risk Report 2024
assets.kpmg.com/content/dam/kpmg/xx/pdf/2024/03/2024-climate-risk-report.pdf

'Climate Scorpion – the sting is in the tail' is the IFoA's third report in collaboration with climate scientists
https://actuaries.org.uk/media/g1qevrfa/climate-scorpion.pdf

Sustainability Action Plans

Drawdown: The Most Comprehensive Plan Ever Proposed to Reverse Global Warming Paperback – 22 Feb. 2018 by Paul Hawken (Author). ISBN 978-0141988436

The Sustainability Handbook: The Complete Management Guide to Achieving Social, Economic and Environmental Responsibility Hardcover – 15 Oct. 2007 by William R. Blackburn (Author). ISBN 978-1844074952

Little Book of Big Eco Actions: Seven Generation Sustainability by Jonathan Frost (Author), GPT 4.0 (Author). ISBN 979-8858067580

Mineral Resources Reports

Simon Michaux

https://www.simonmichaux.com/gtk-reports

Printed in Great Britain
by Amazon